AF504902

LAST SUMMER

PHILIPP KEEL
LAST SUMMER

STEIDL

CONTENTS

7

PREFACE

8

PLATES

69

LIST OF WORKS

The most beautiful summers are often also the most painful.
We rarely feel more alive. And at the end of those summers, we're
reminded all the more strongly that everything passes. Looking
at Philipp Keel's new works for "Last Summer", I notice the ab-
sence – apart from a nude – of people. Instead, there are still lifes
and above all pictures of palms, pools, drinks, initially seeming
cool and summery, plus many captured moments and incidental
poetry. Common to them all is the artist's eye for specific details
and moods, and yet on closer inspection we can sense the melancholy permeating many of his works. At times, the moment
has already passed or is only visible on the blurred margins of our
consciousness. What remains is a feeling of transience, perhaps
even a faint touch of loneliness.

One of the great strengths of these works is that the pictures stay
subtle and reserved. We each find in them what we wish to find.
In some, the melancholy is light-hearted, little more than a gentle,
not unpleasant tug at a taut string somewhere deep inside us.
Yet in others there is more to it. "Last Summer" takes us to a
threshold. Evening has set in, a solitary view from a veranda with
a drink in hand, friends laughing in the background as the day's
last light fades. In our mind play the images of a day that passed
far too quickly, some flickering, some clear. Perhaps we feel briefly
wistful, or perhaps we turn around and go back to the others.

Benedict Wells

Palm Leaves II, 2019

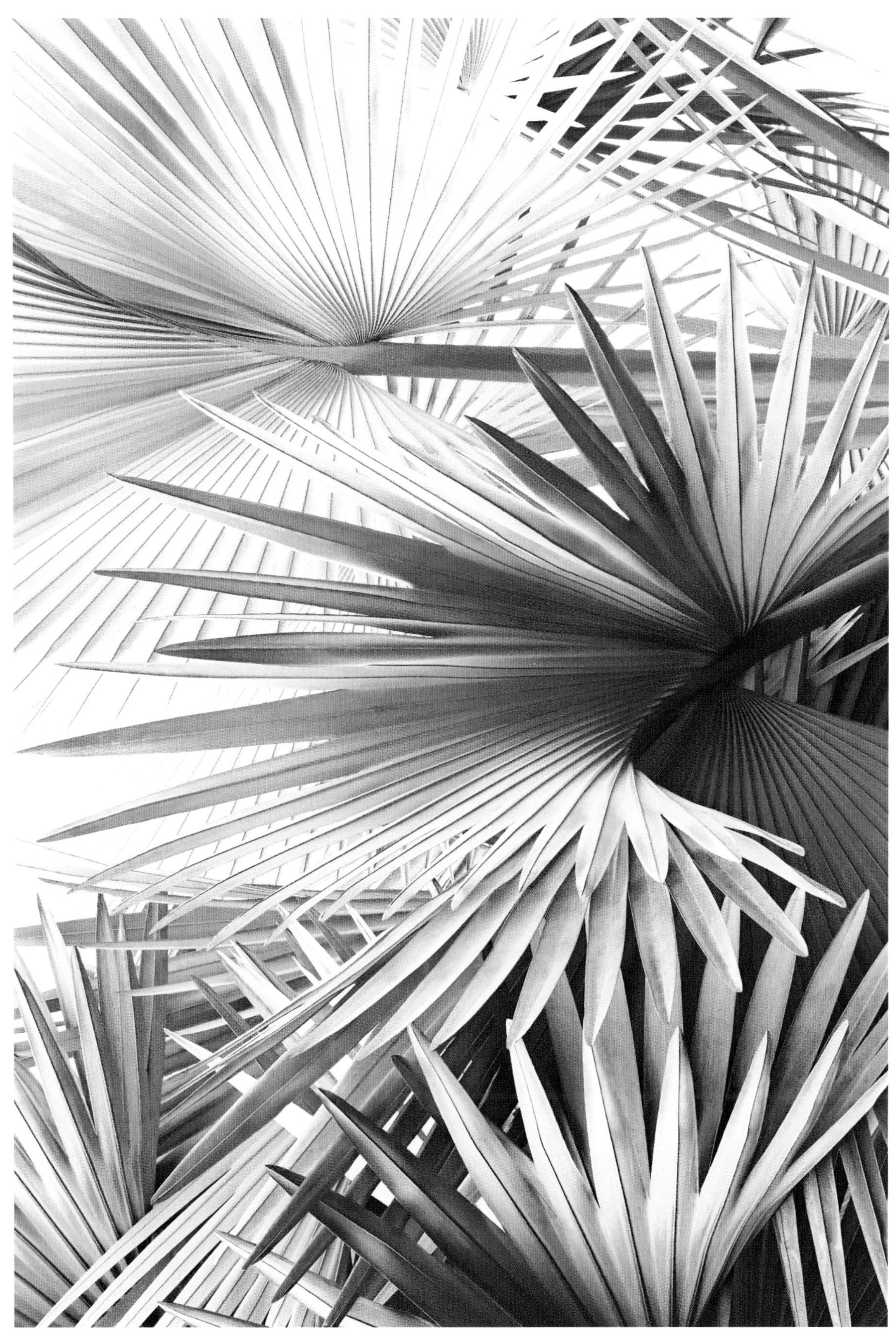

Osaka Umbrella, 2017

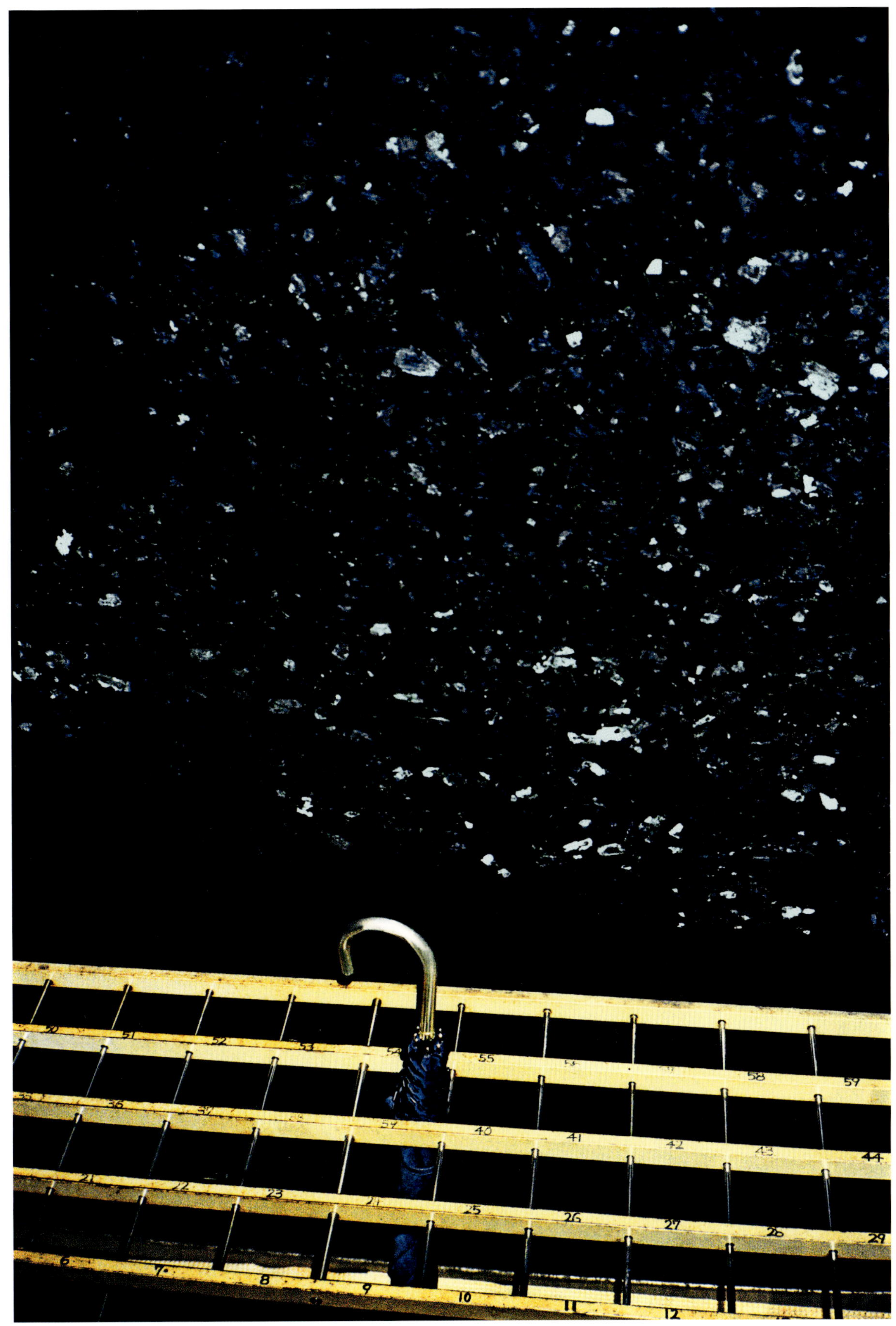

Sea, 2017

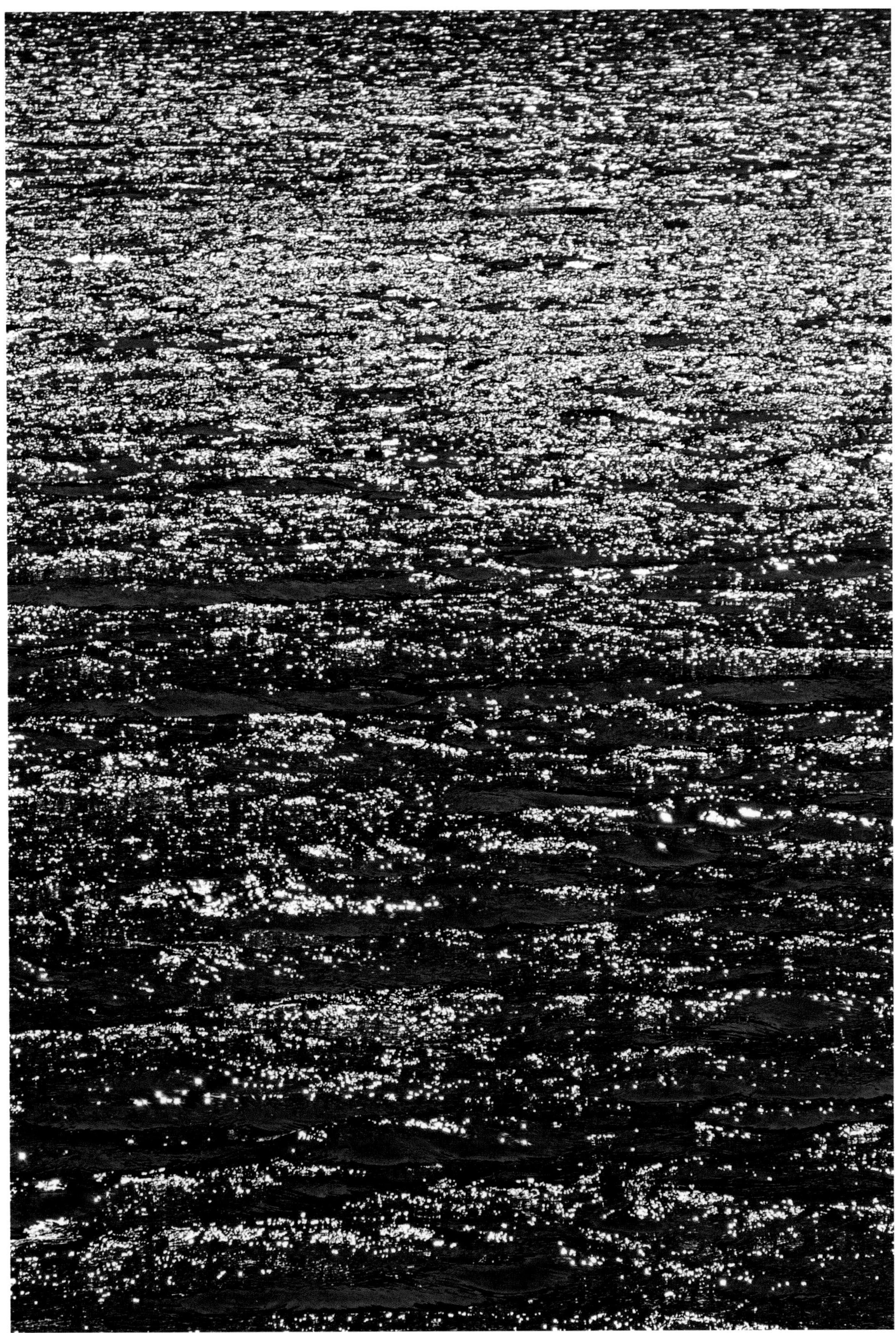

Tarifa, 2018

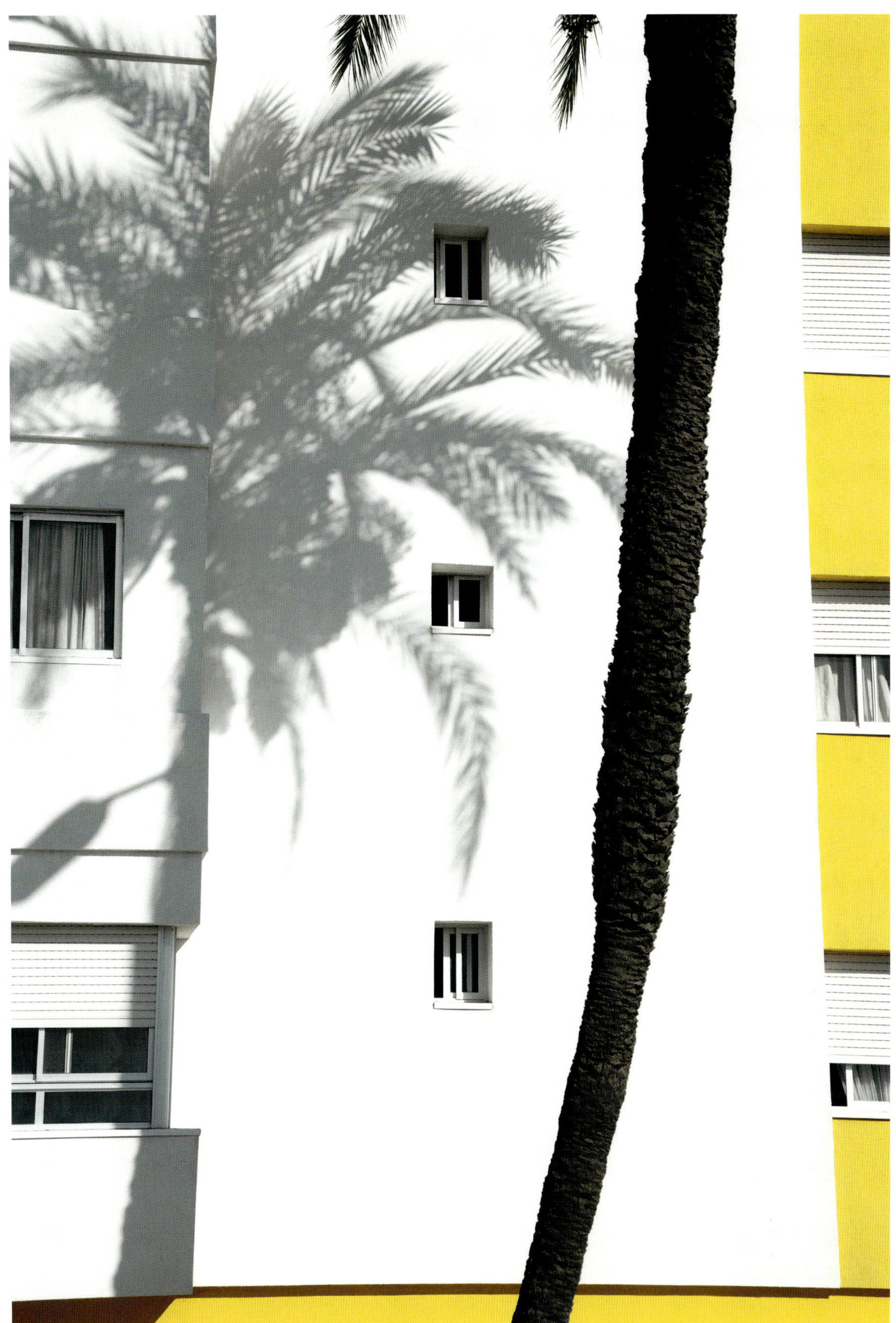

Pink Cloud, 2018

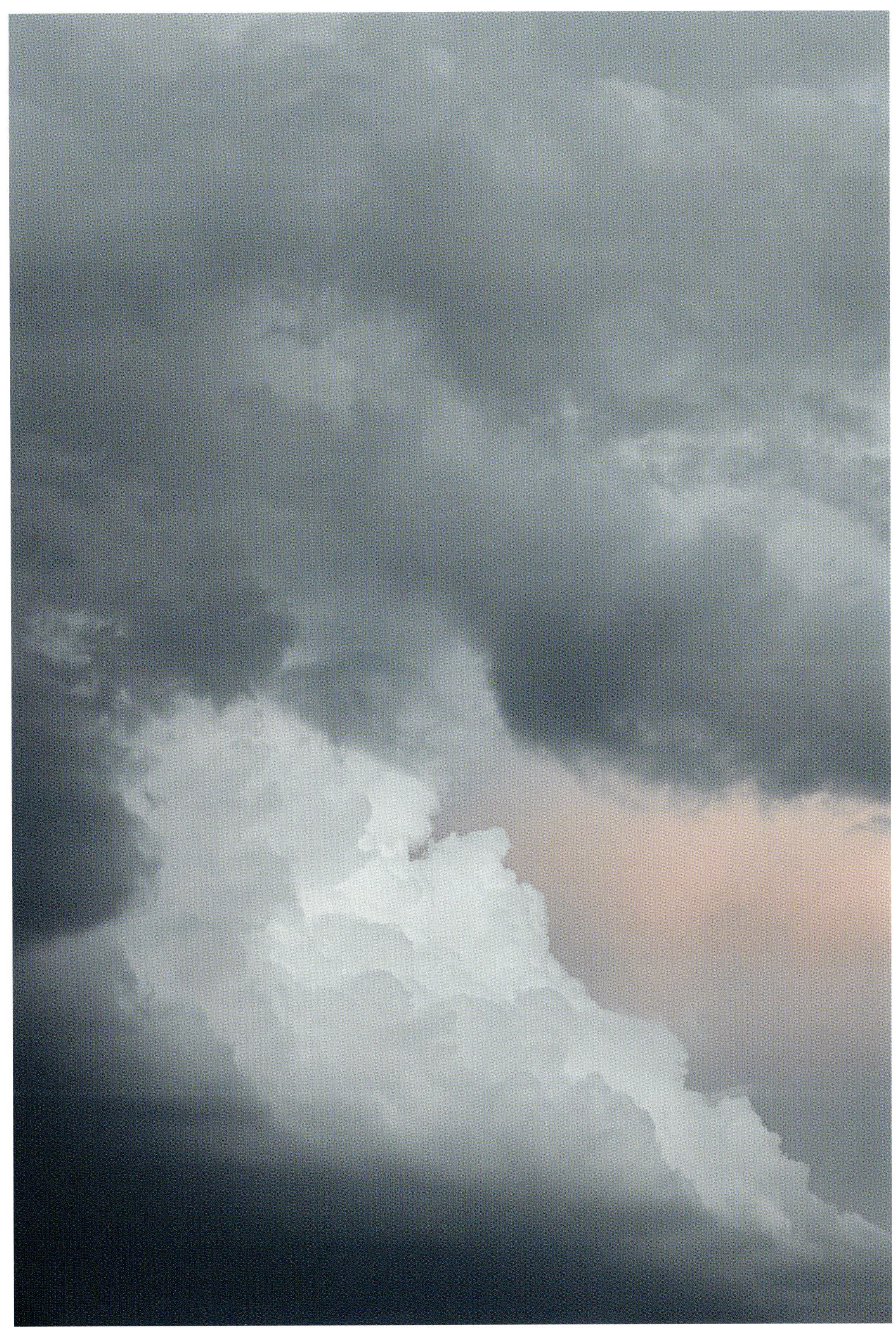

Empire State Building II, 2018

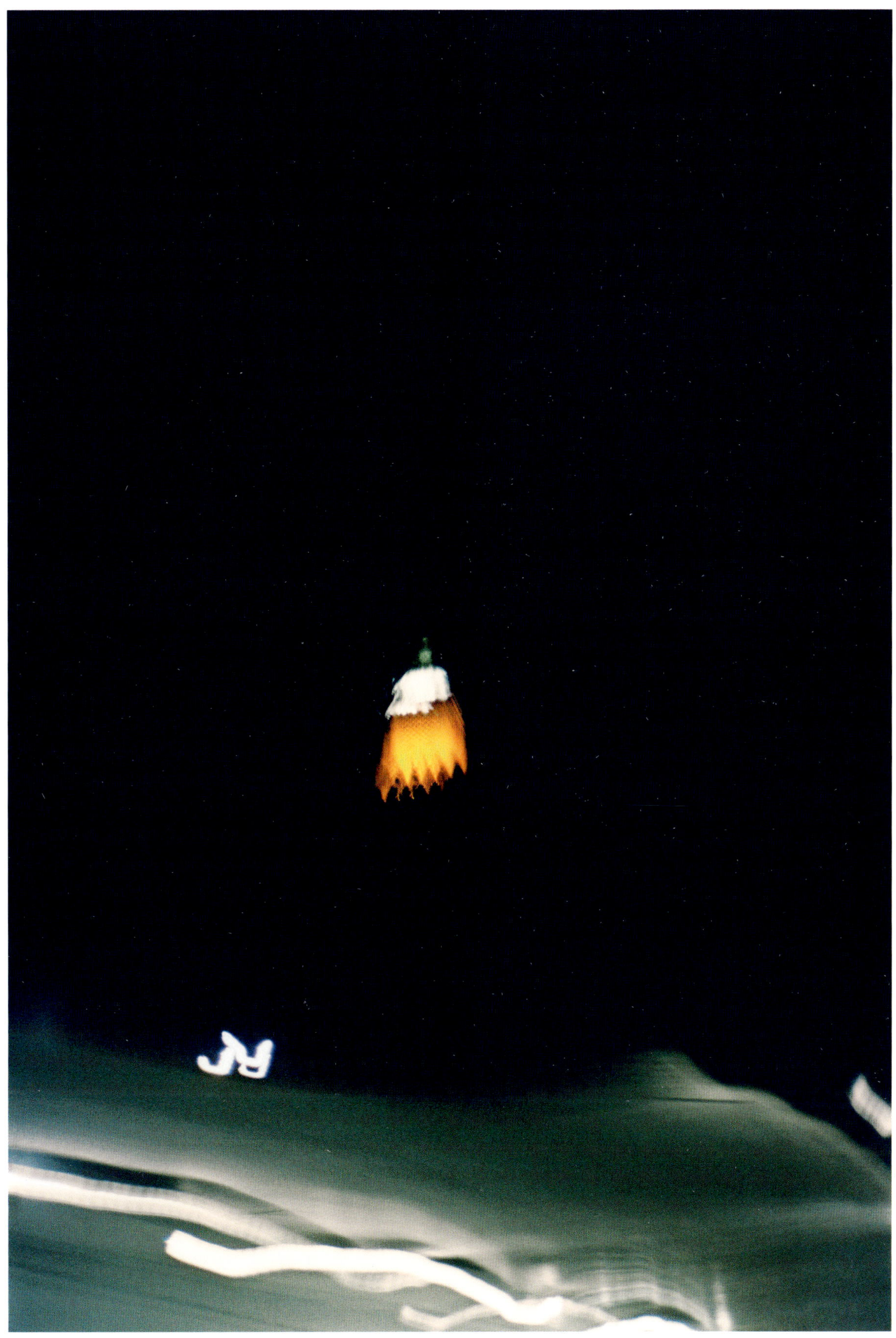

Wire Tree, 2017

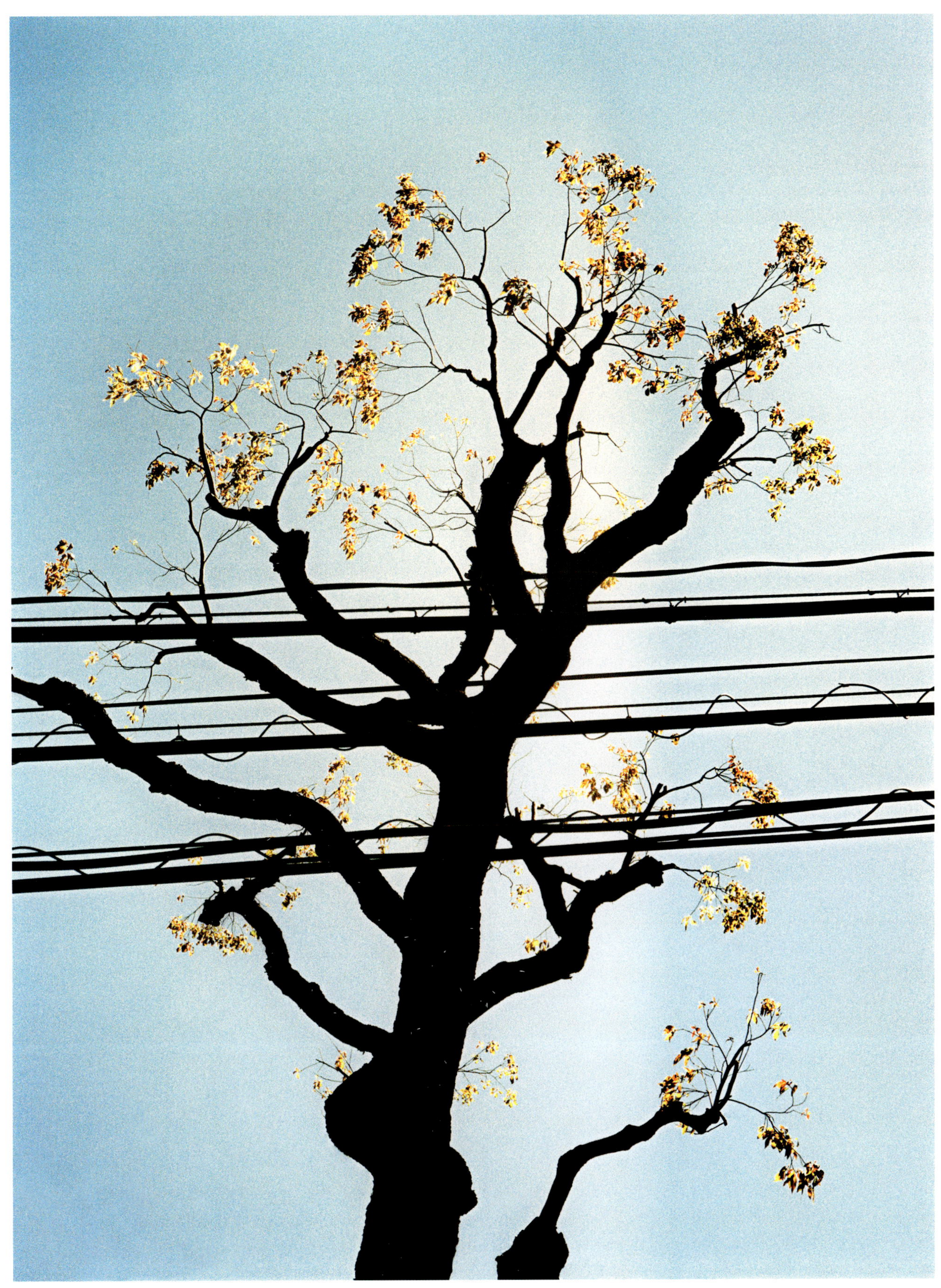

Light Switch, 2018

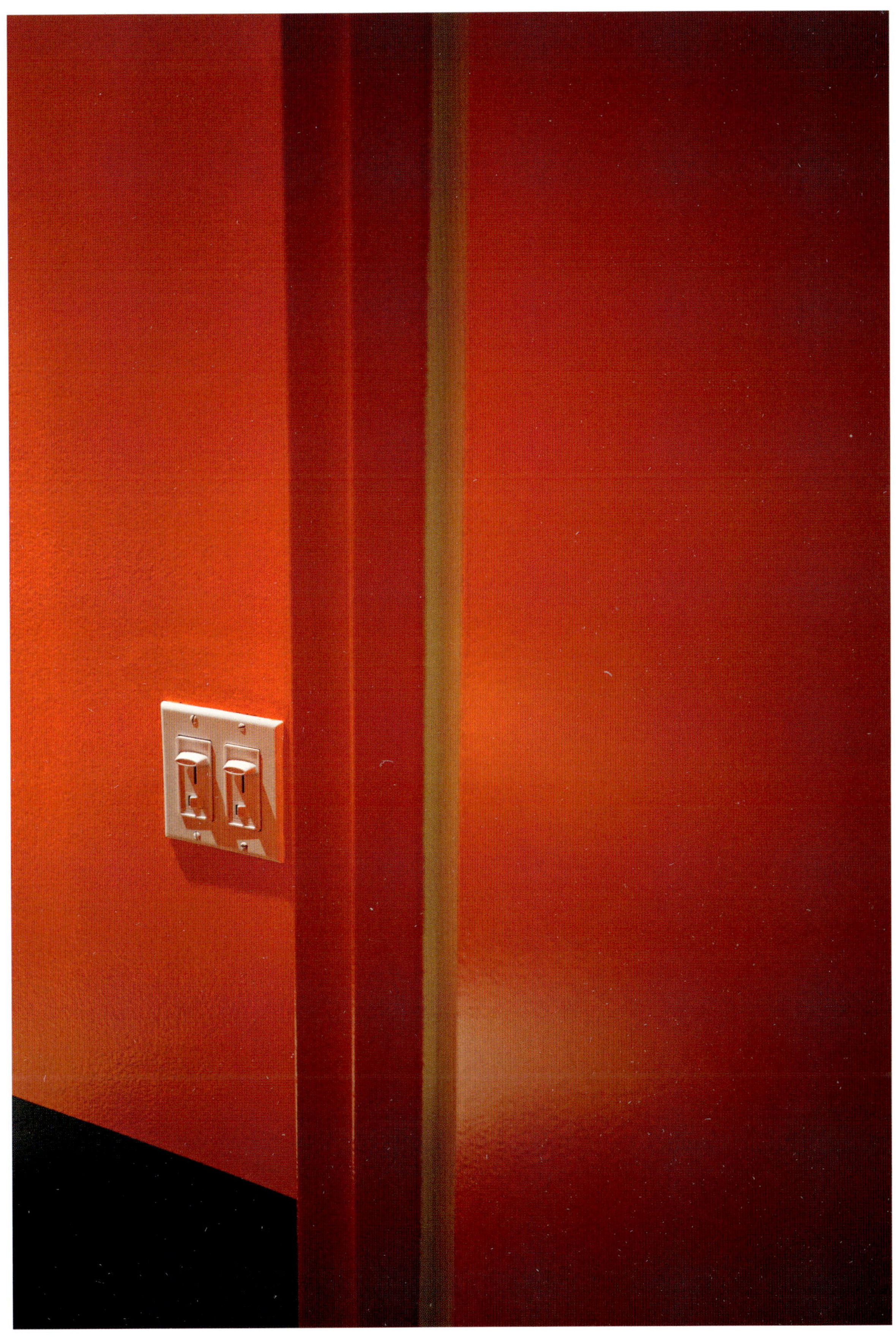

'One must maintain
a little bit of summer,
even in the middle of winter.'

Henry David Thoreau

Palm and a Palm Leaf, 2019

Fender II, 2017

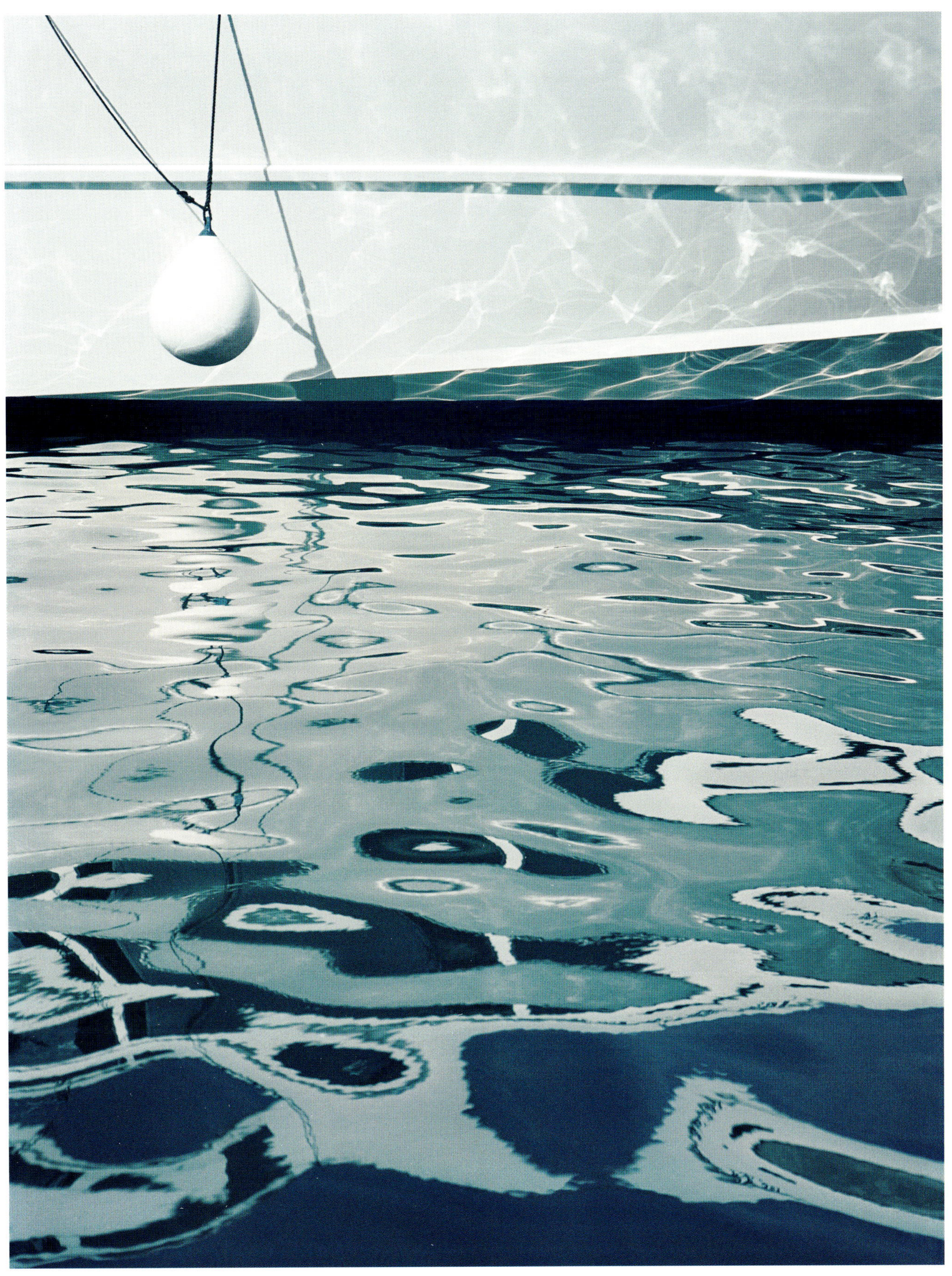

Desk Phone, 2017

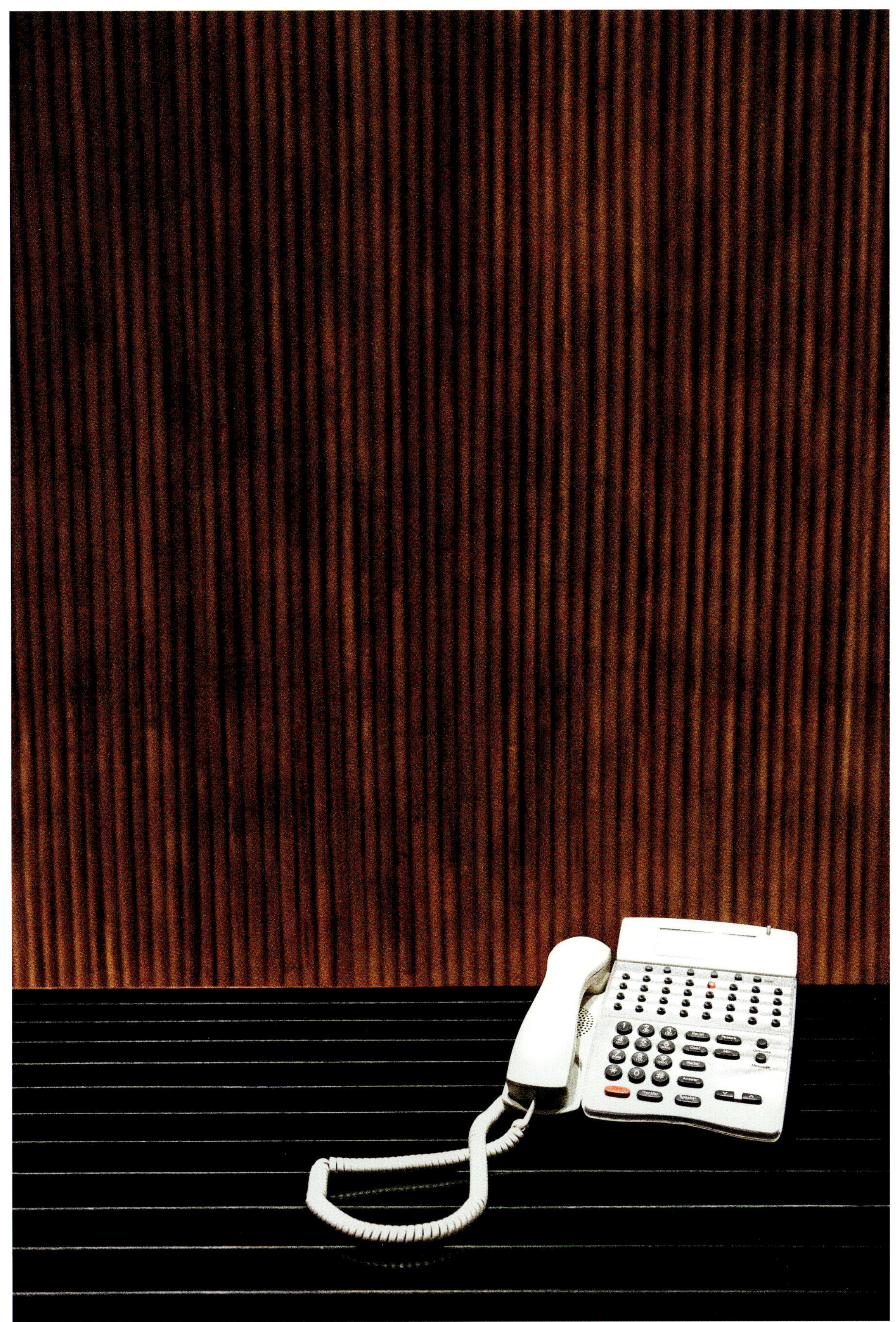

Night Cloud, 2019

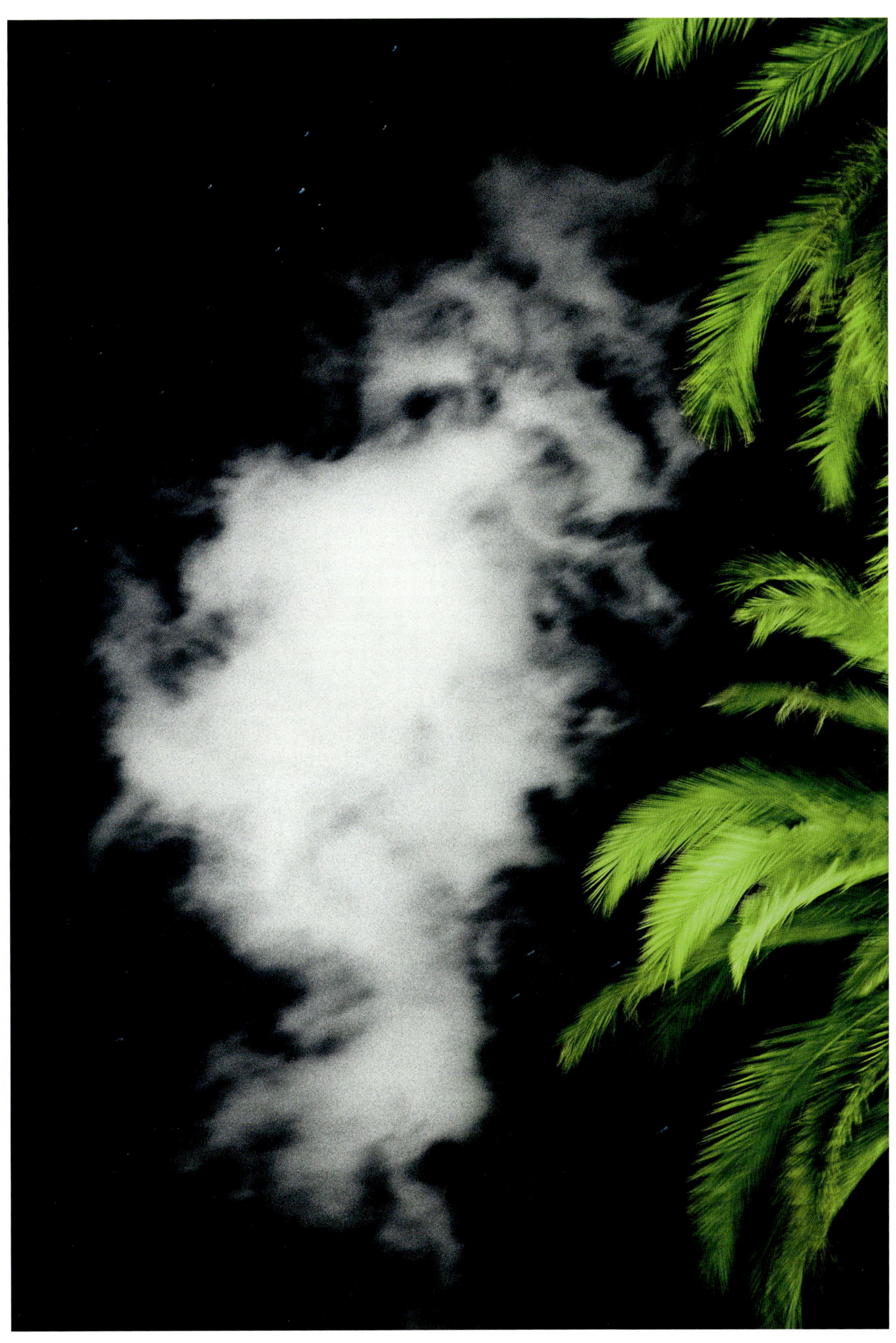

Cherry, 2019

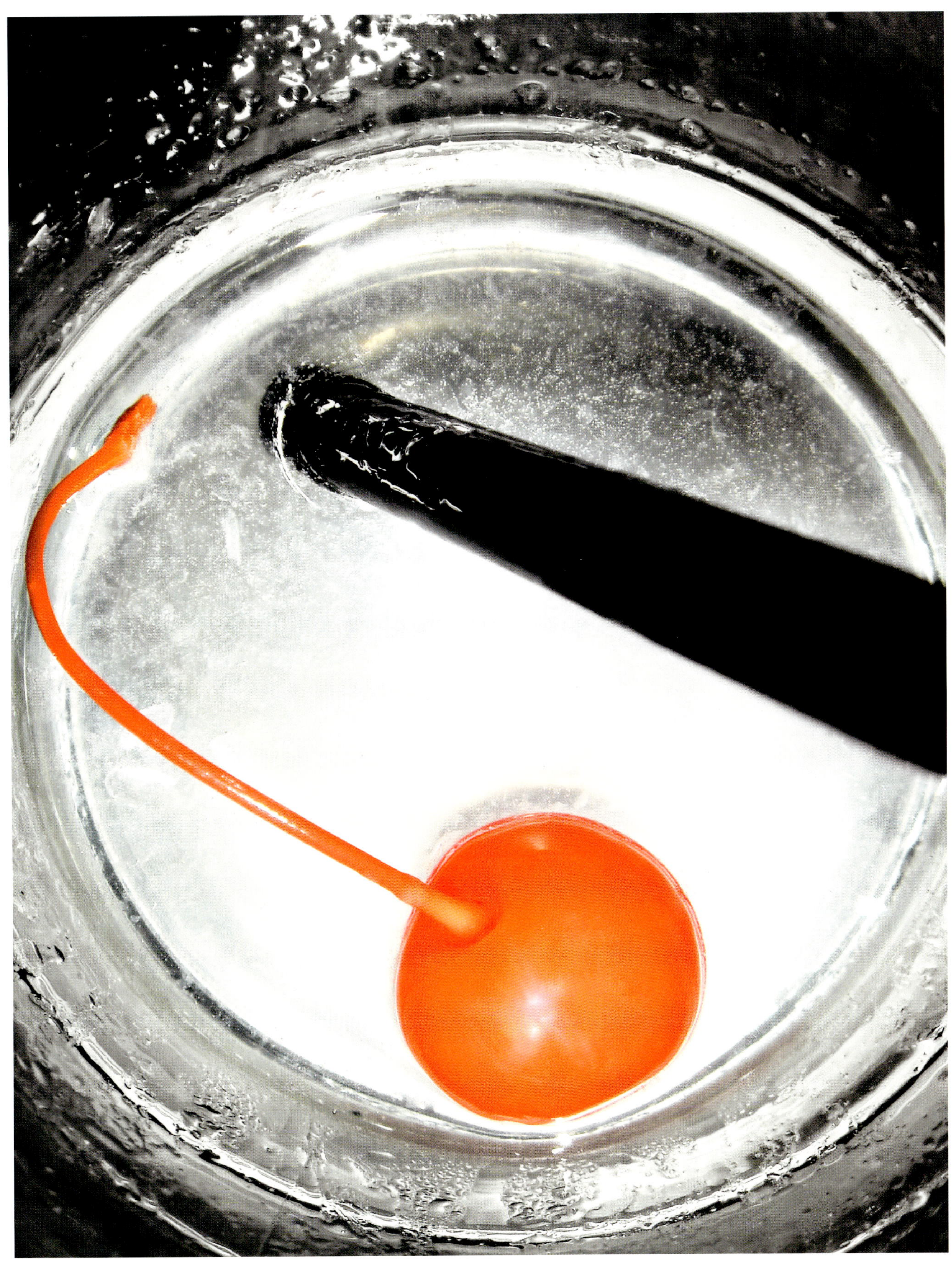

Sunchairs at Night, 2018

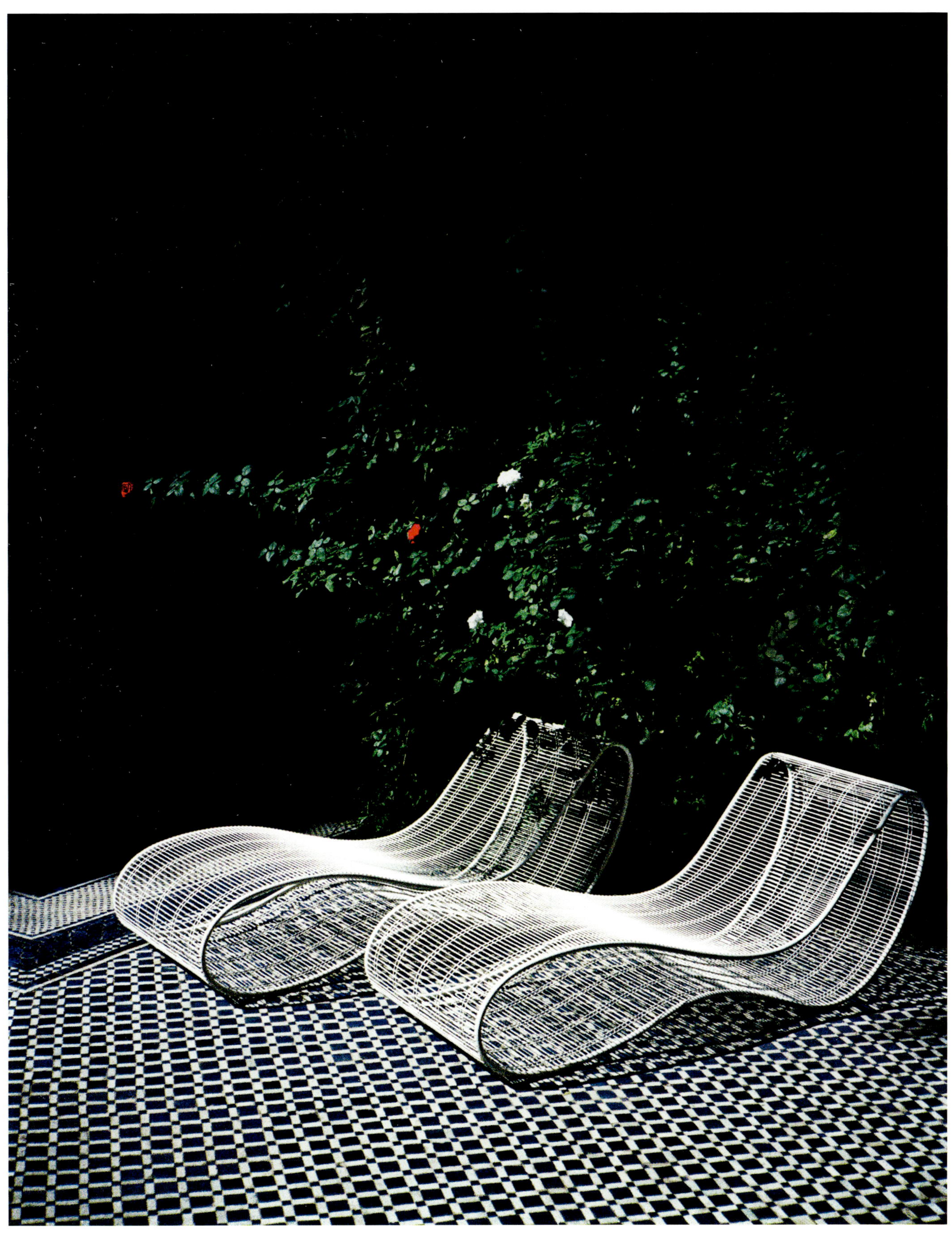

Julie, 2014

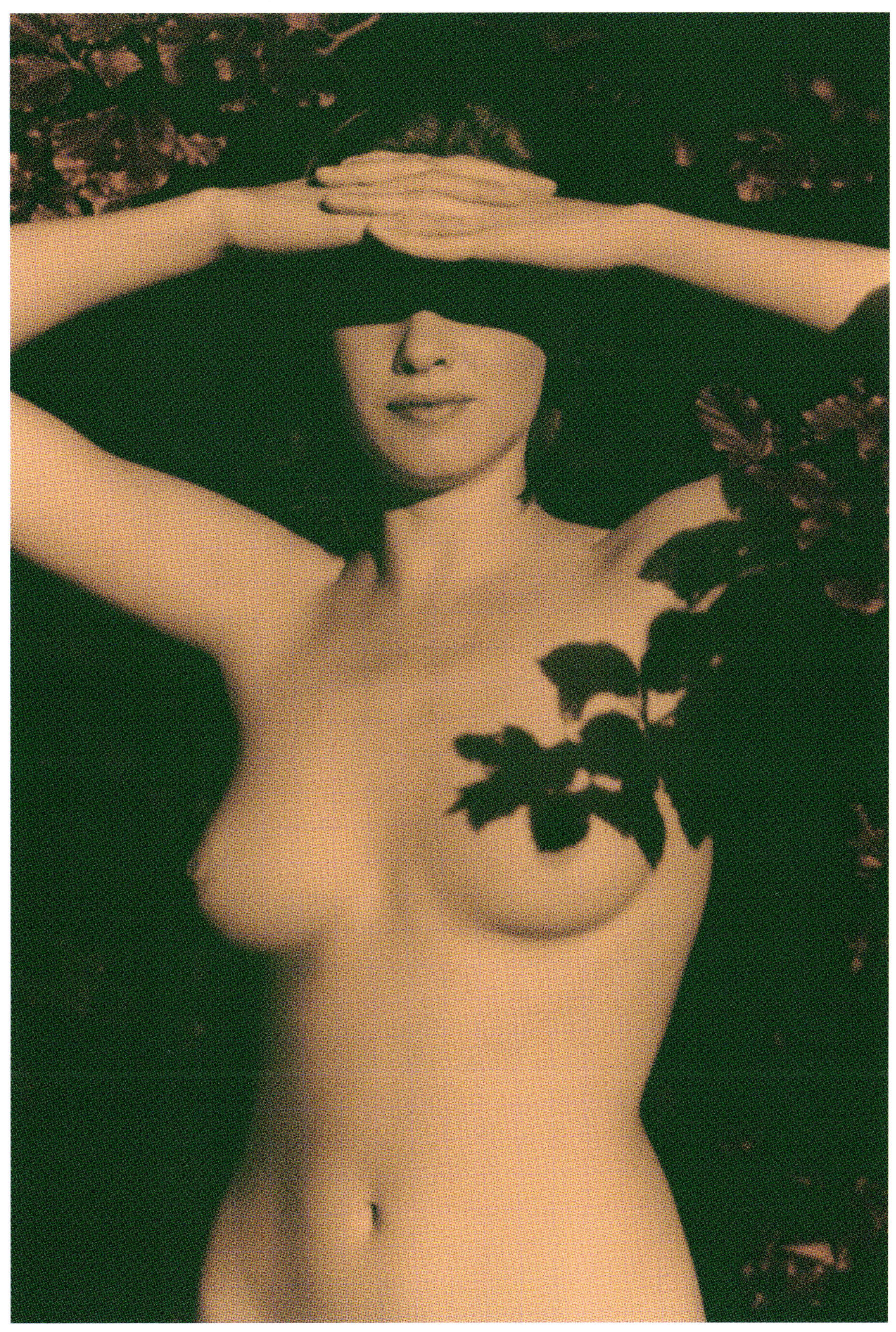

Wave under a Full Moon, 2015

'Live in the sunshine,
swim the sea,
drink the wild air.'

Ralph Waldo Emerson

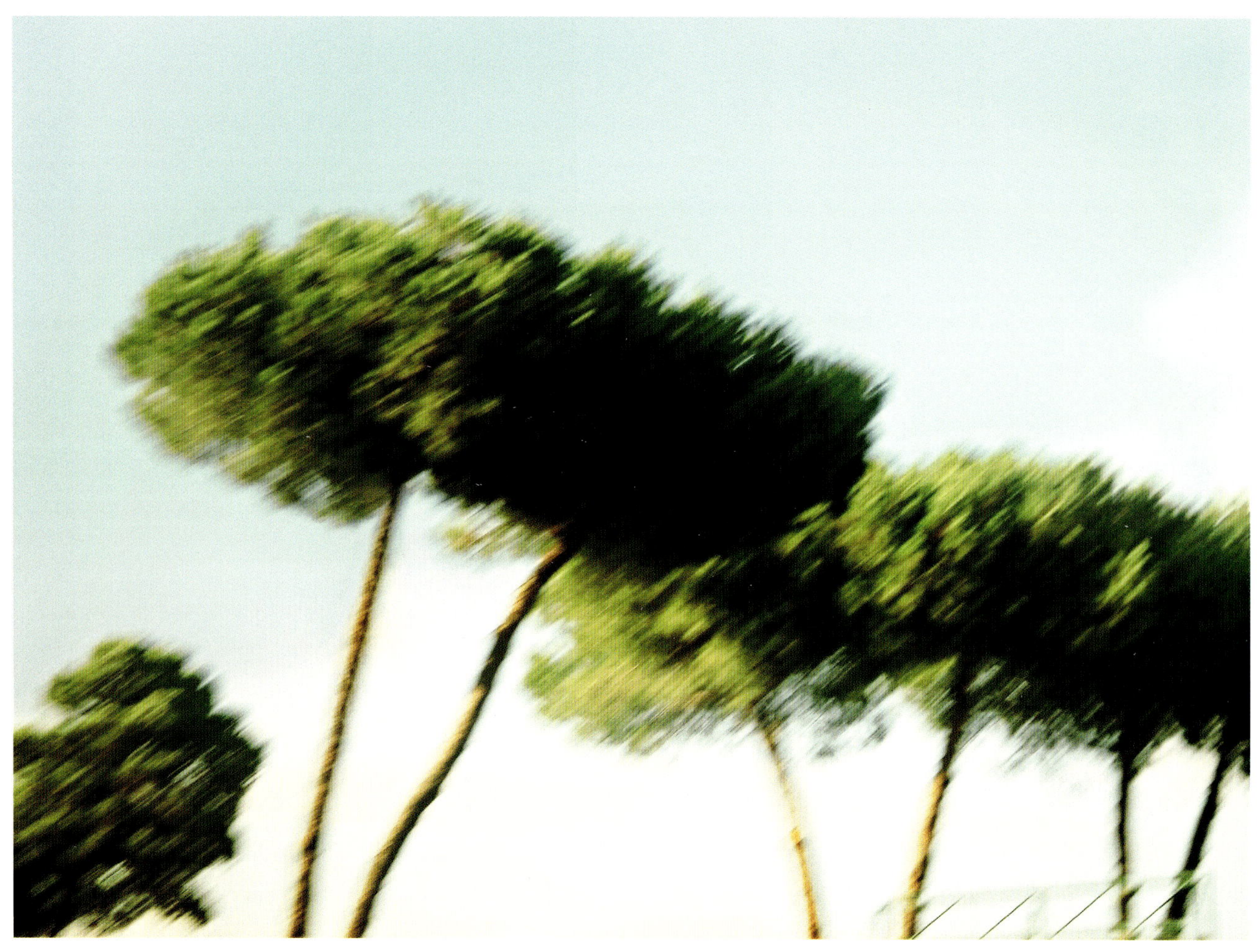

Pine Trees, 2018

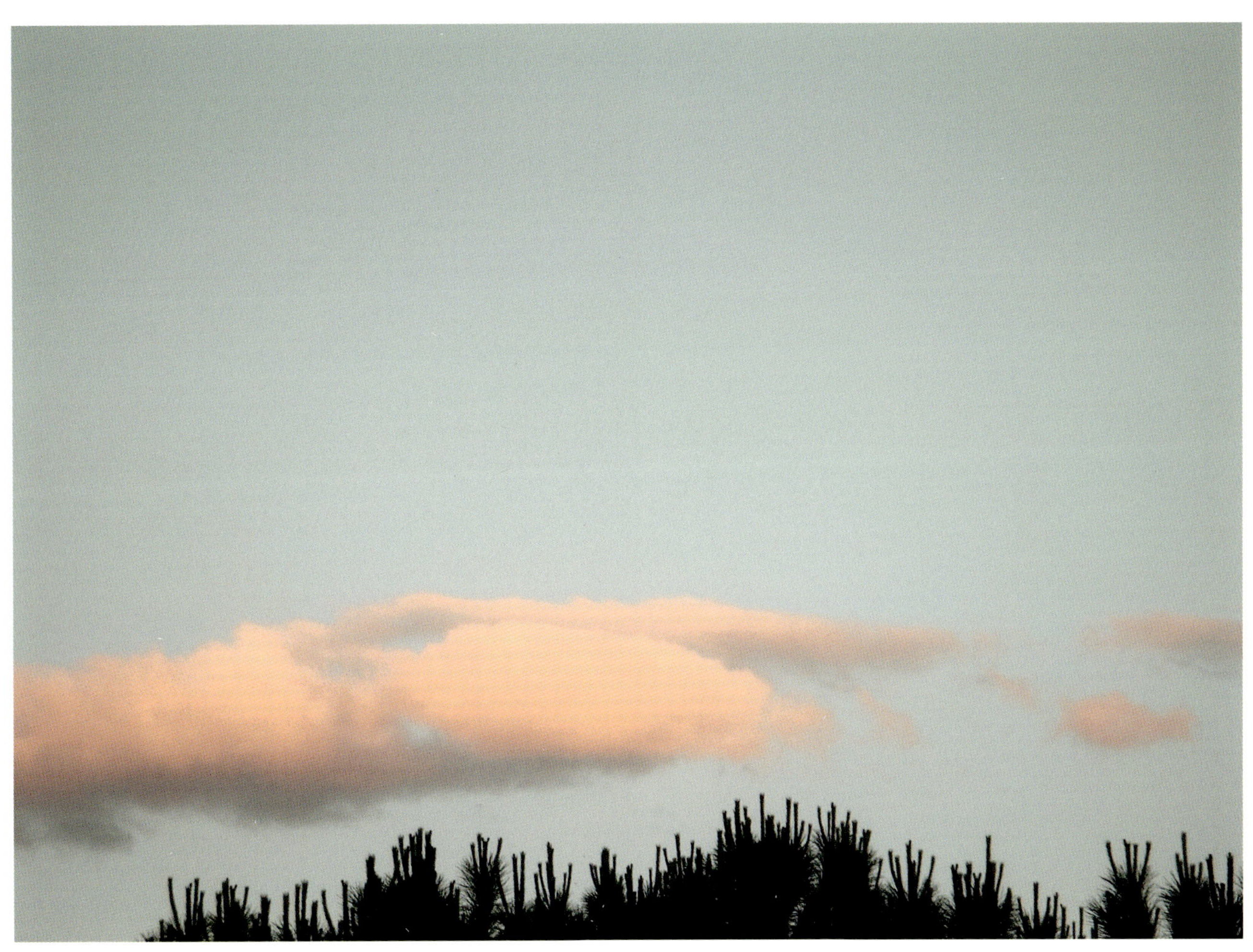

Via Appia, 2018

Business Center, 2017

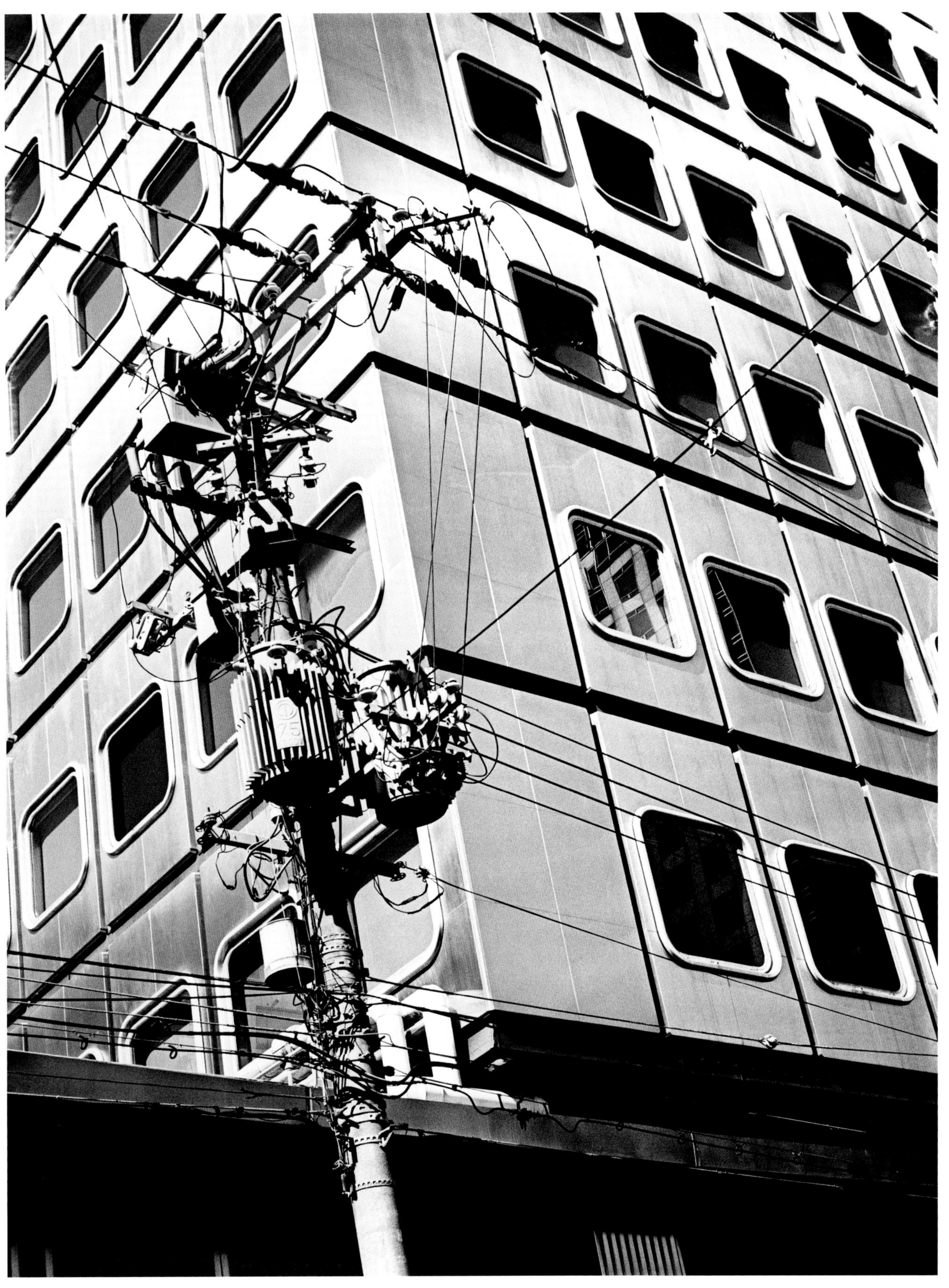

A peach, a plum and a strawberry, 2019

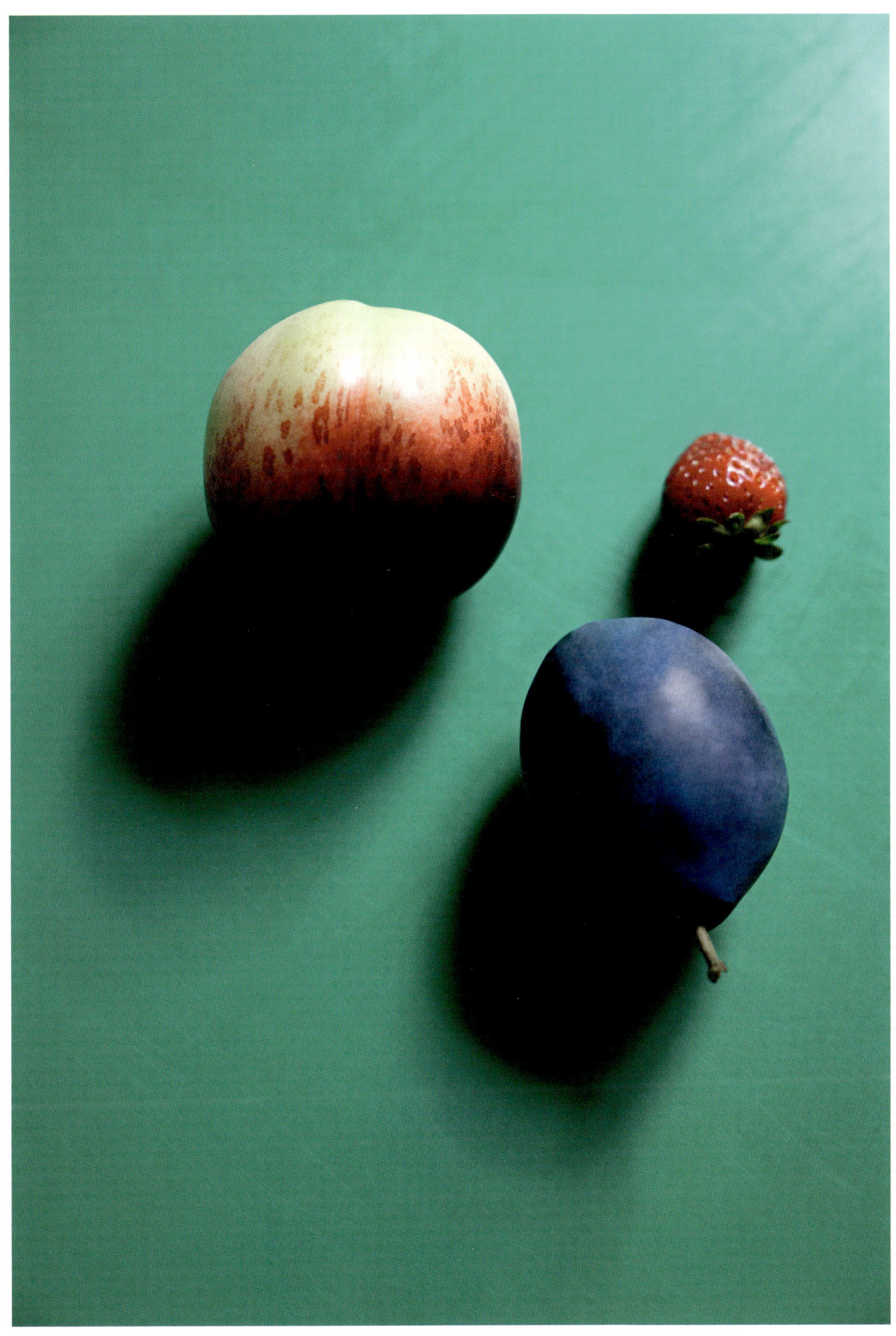

Vacuum Hose, 2019

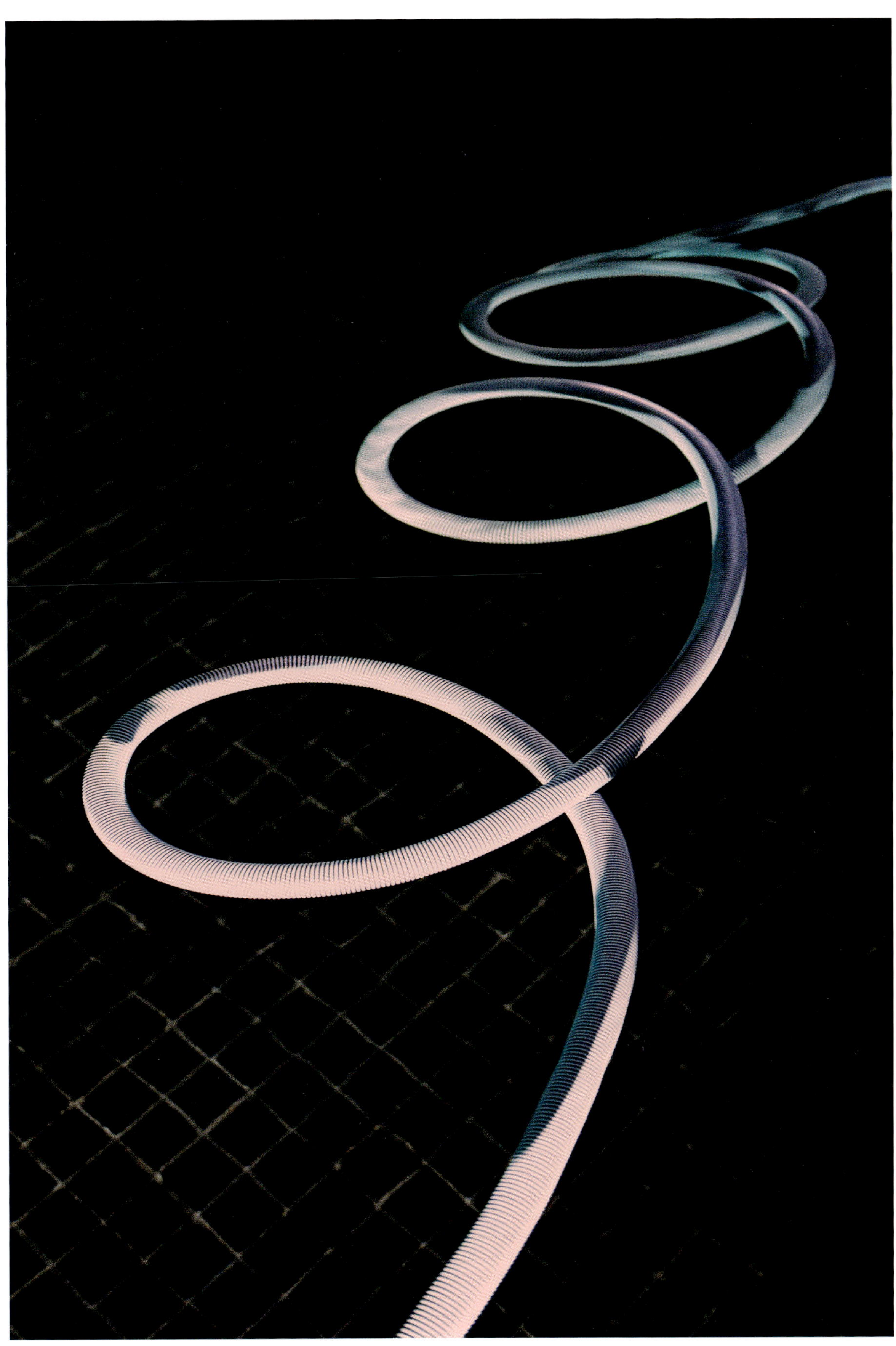

Seville, 2018

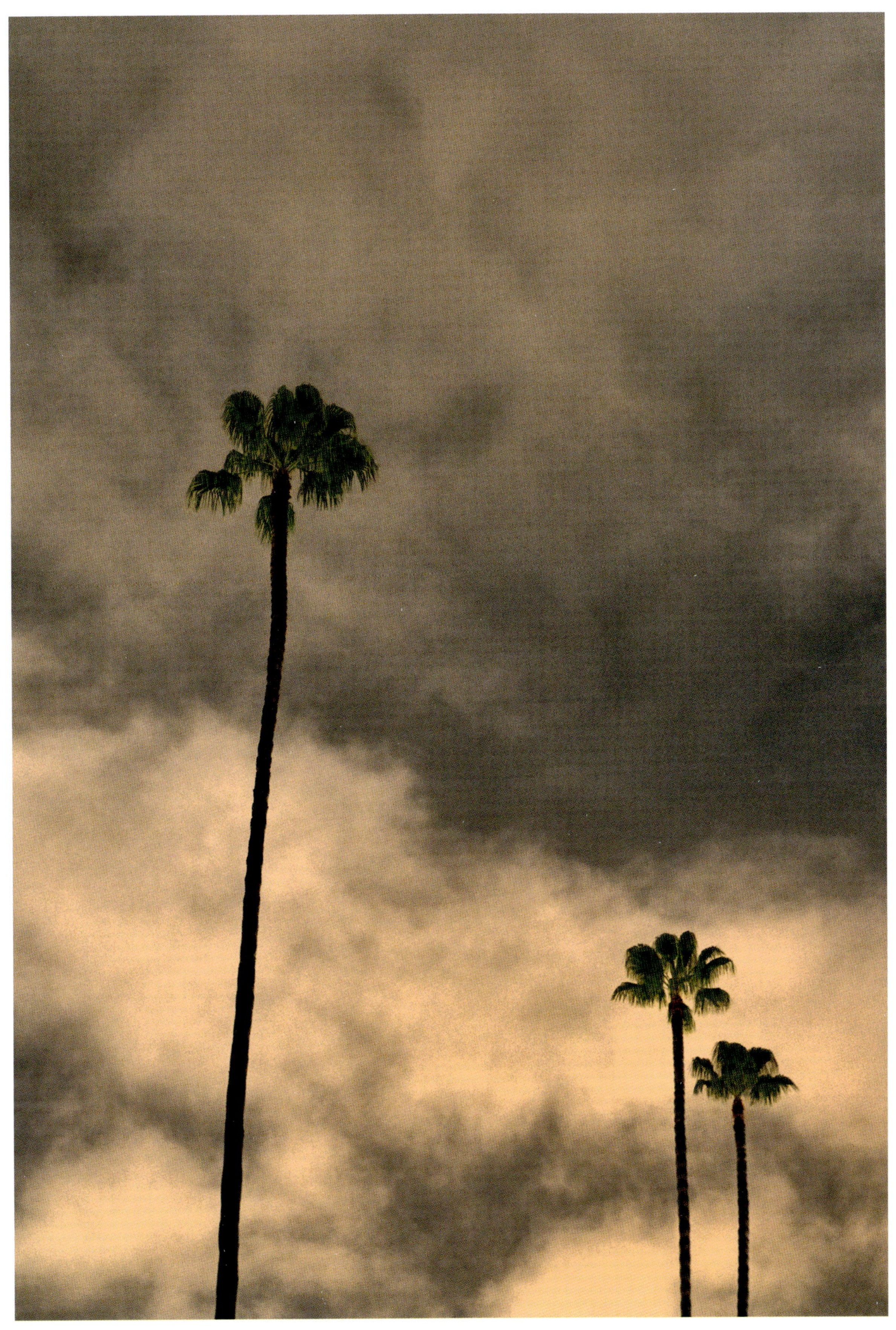

Peonies, a turquoise vase and a blue chair, 2010

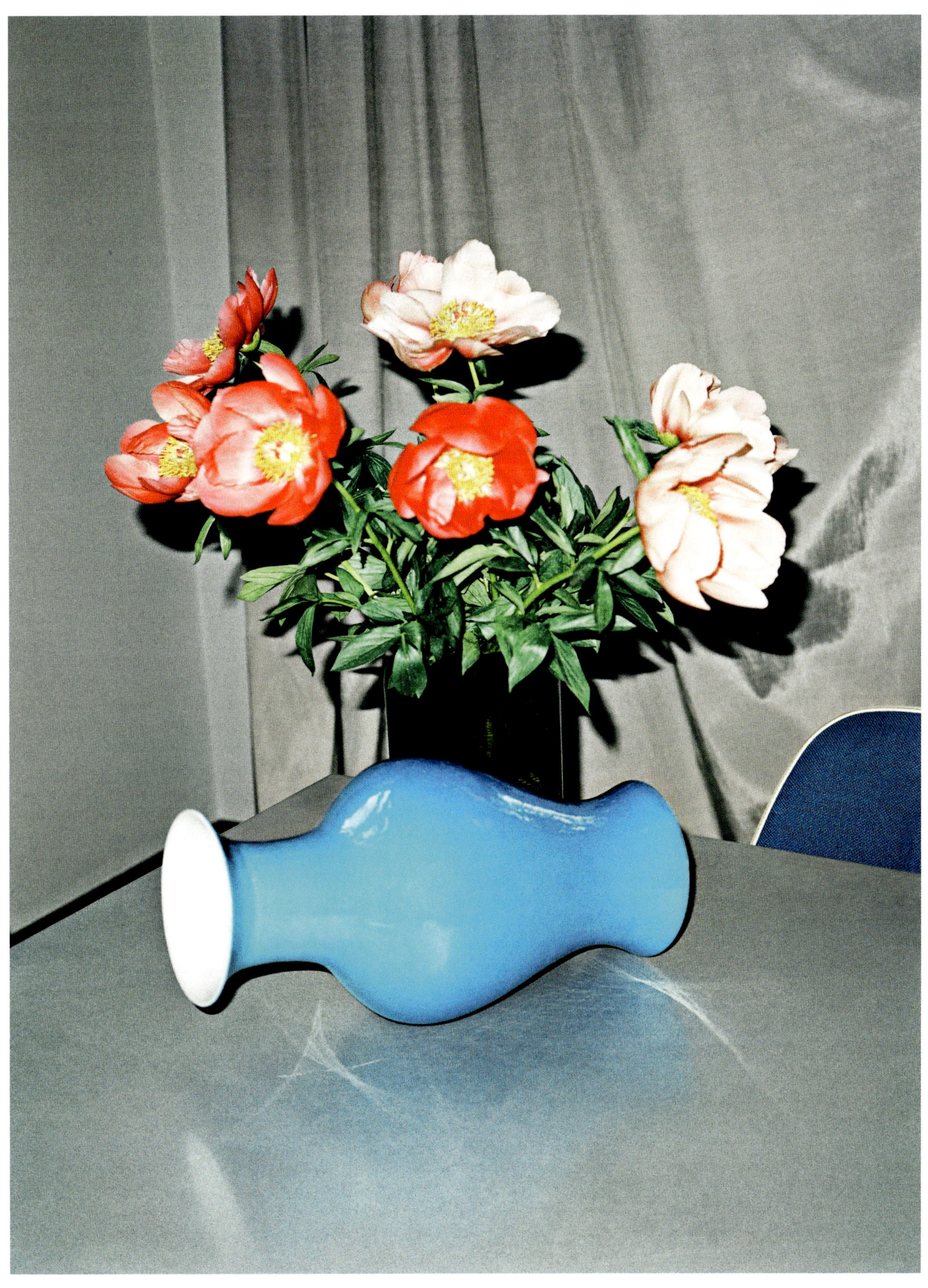

Ray-Ban Series, Four, 2006

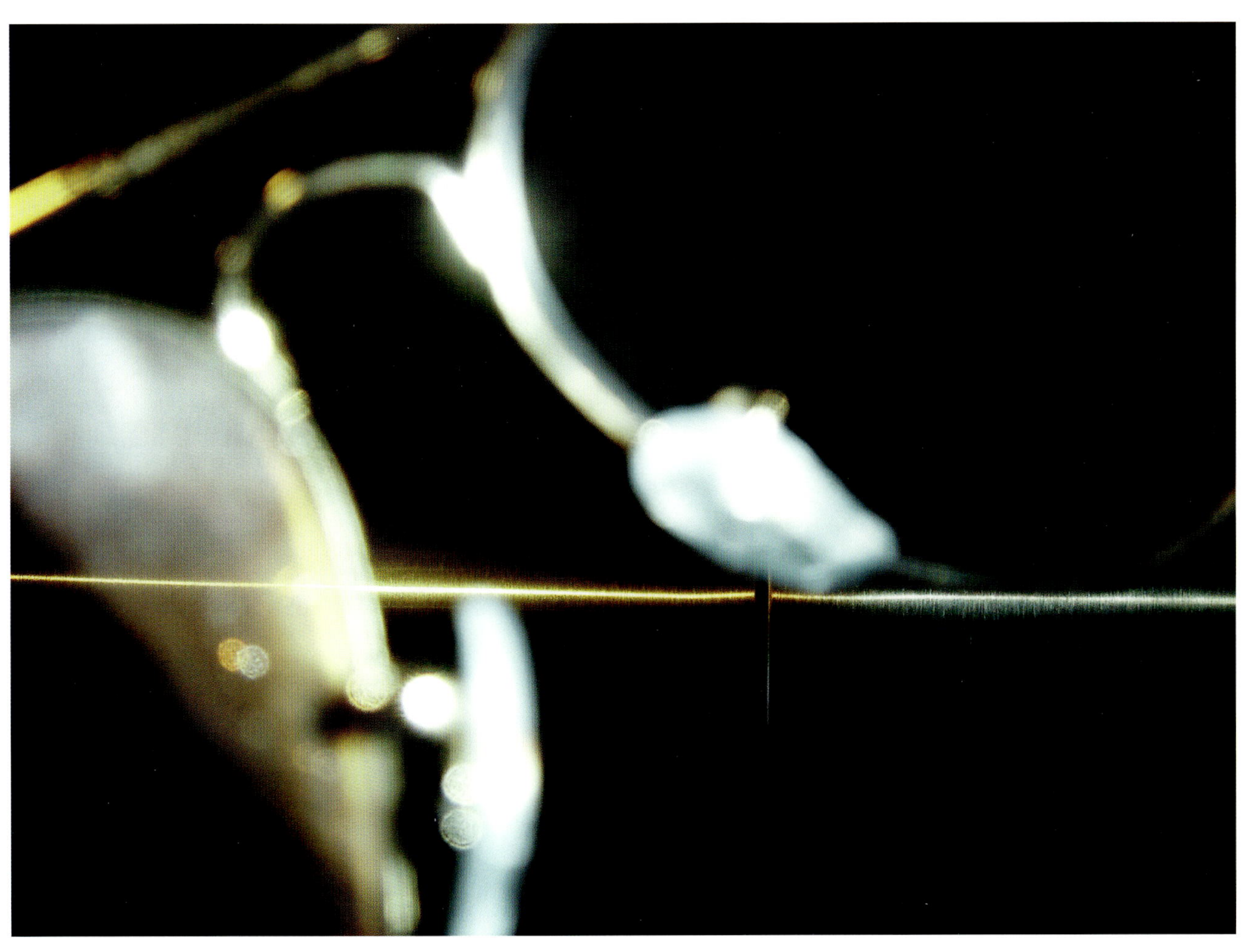

Palms in a Pool, 2017

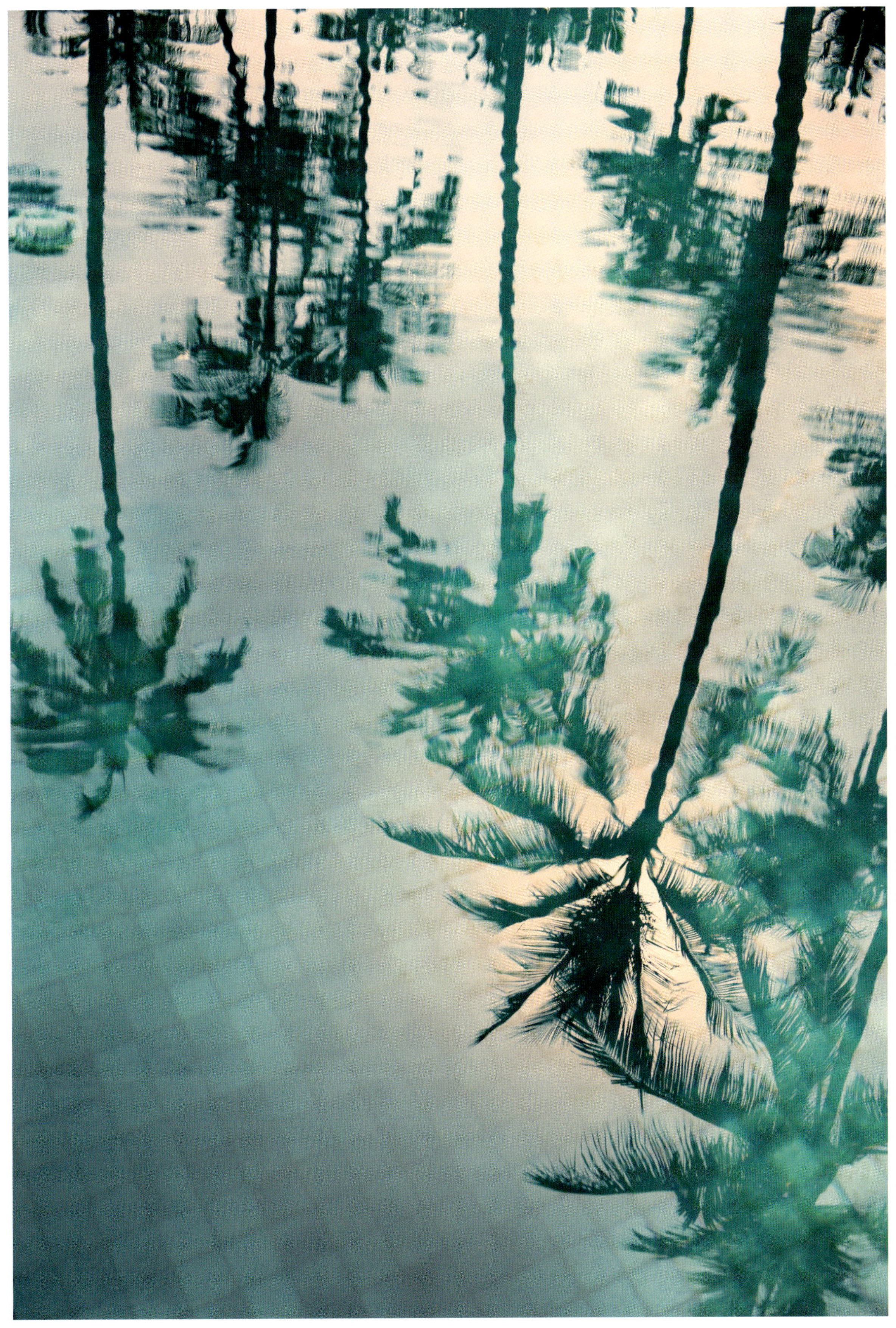

Wynn, 2017

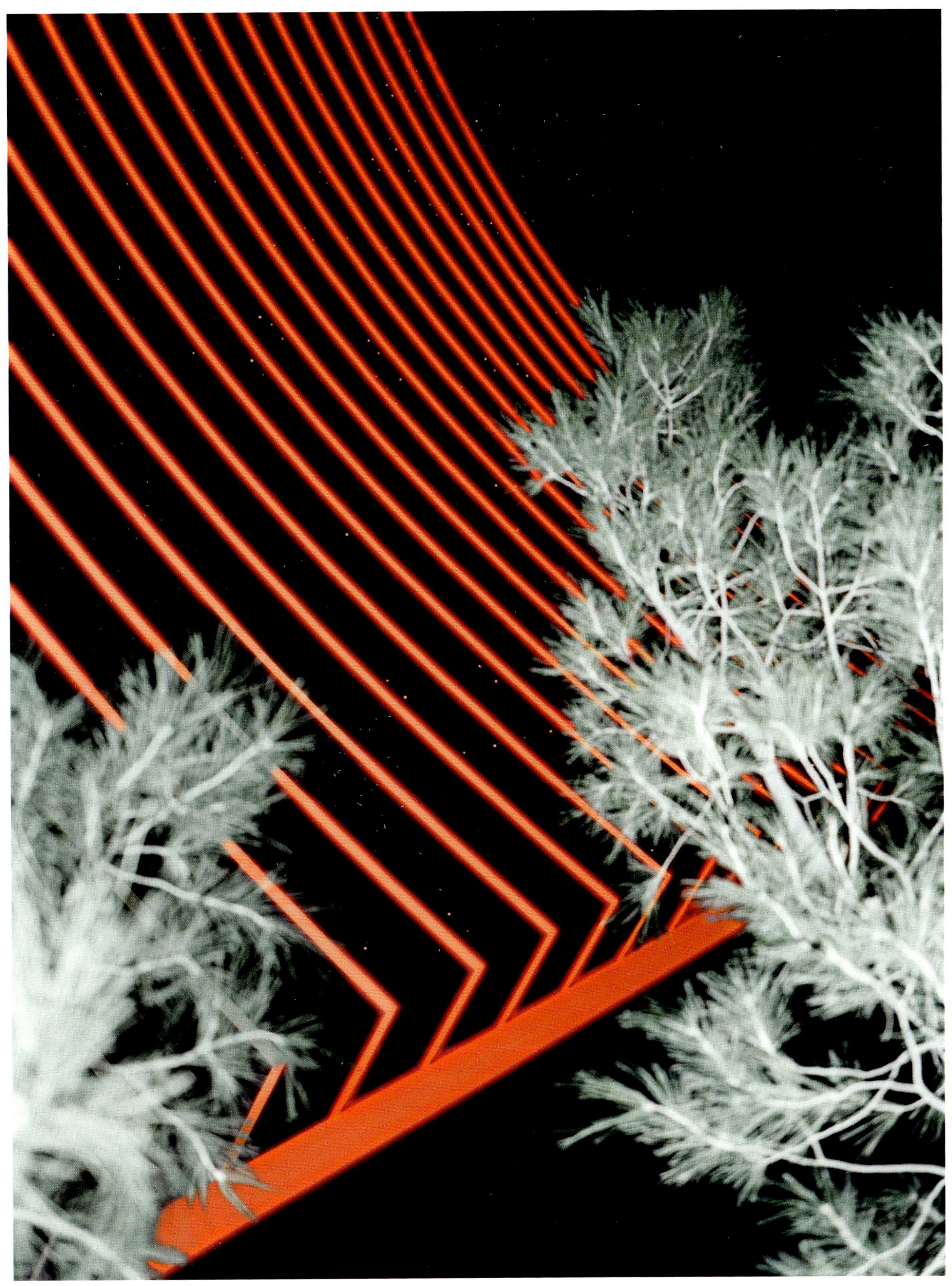

Hay Bales, 2019

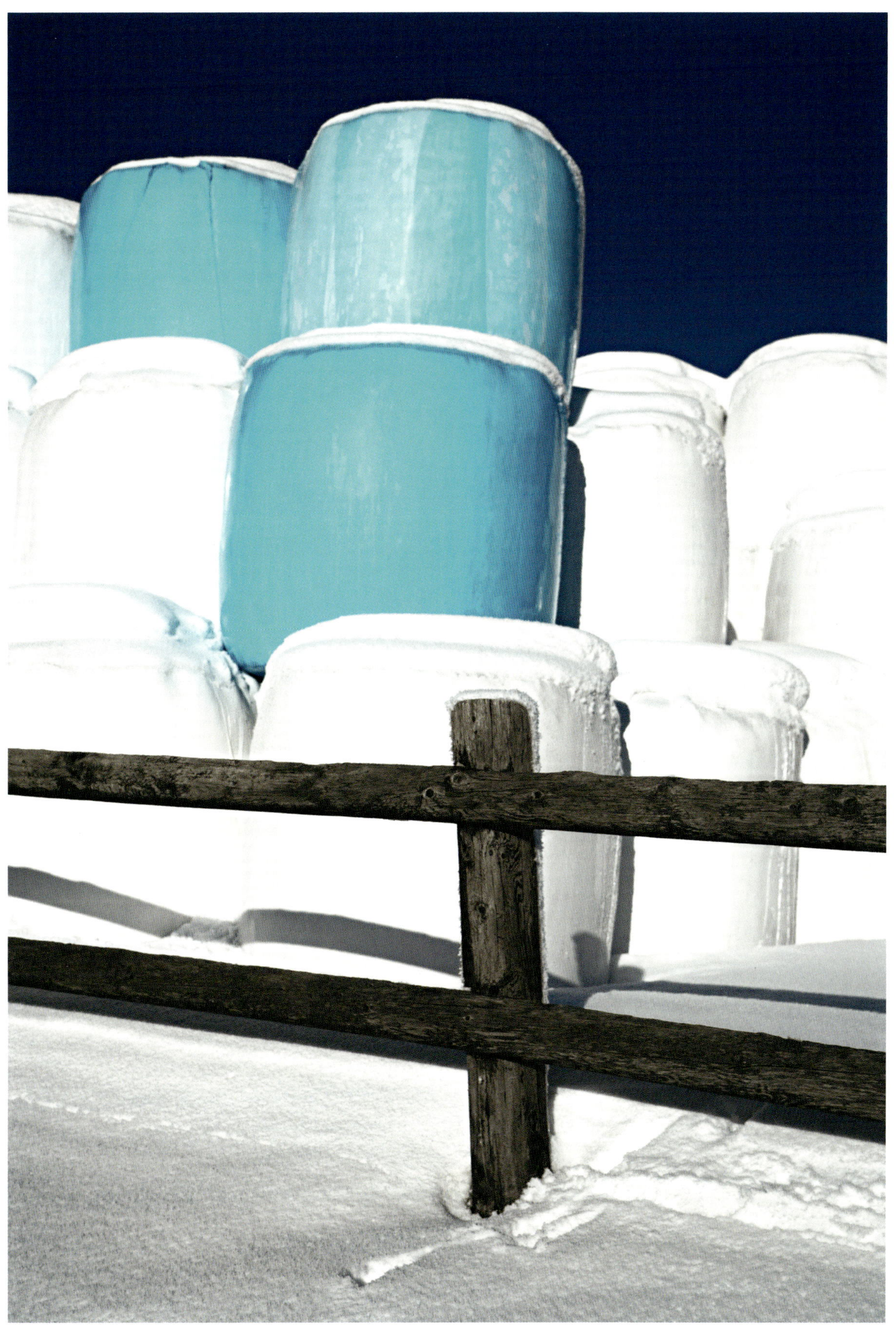

Still Life, 2010

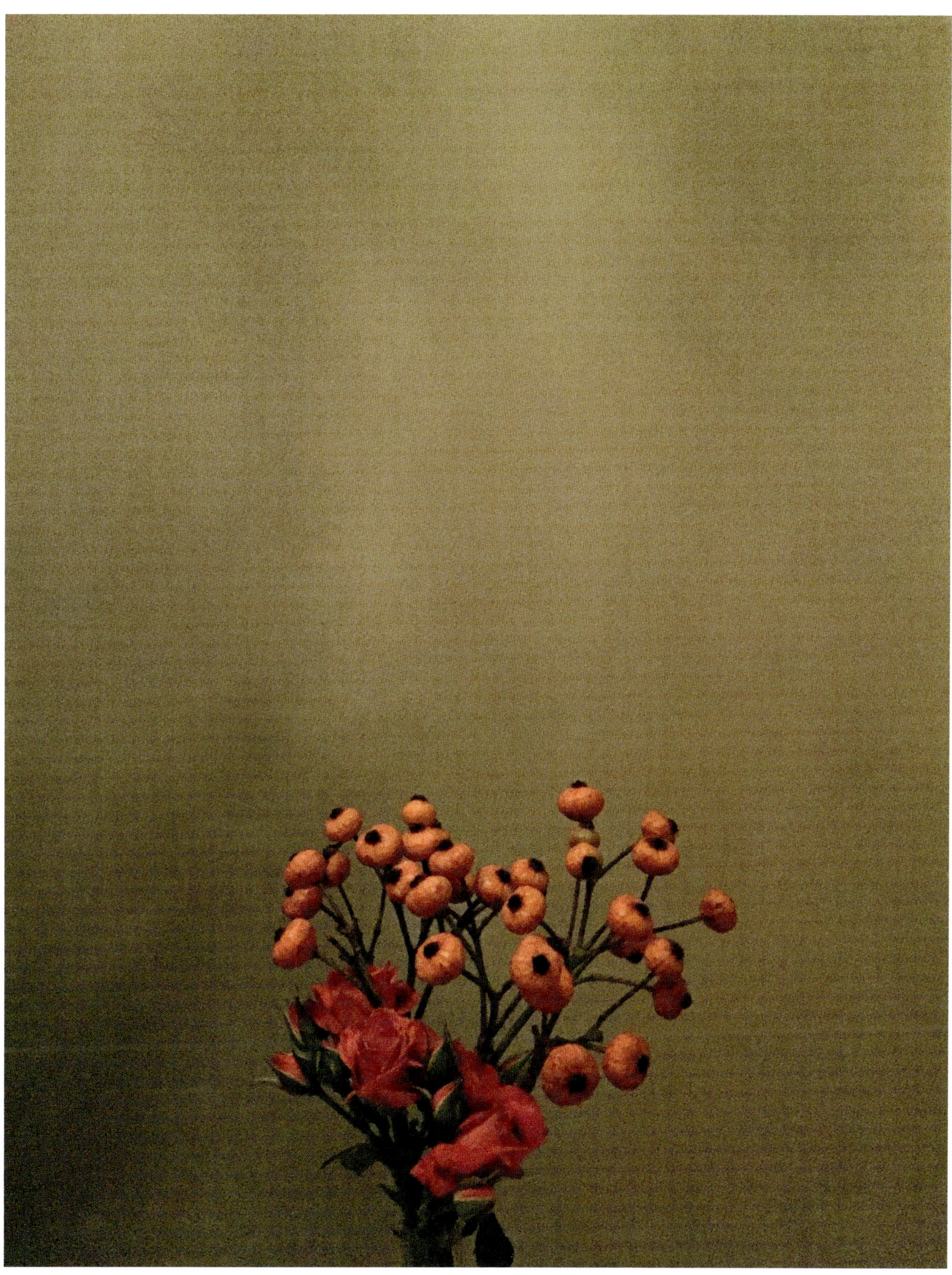

Nippon Tree, 2017

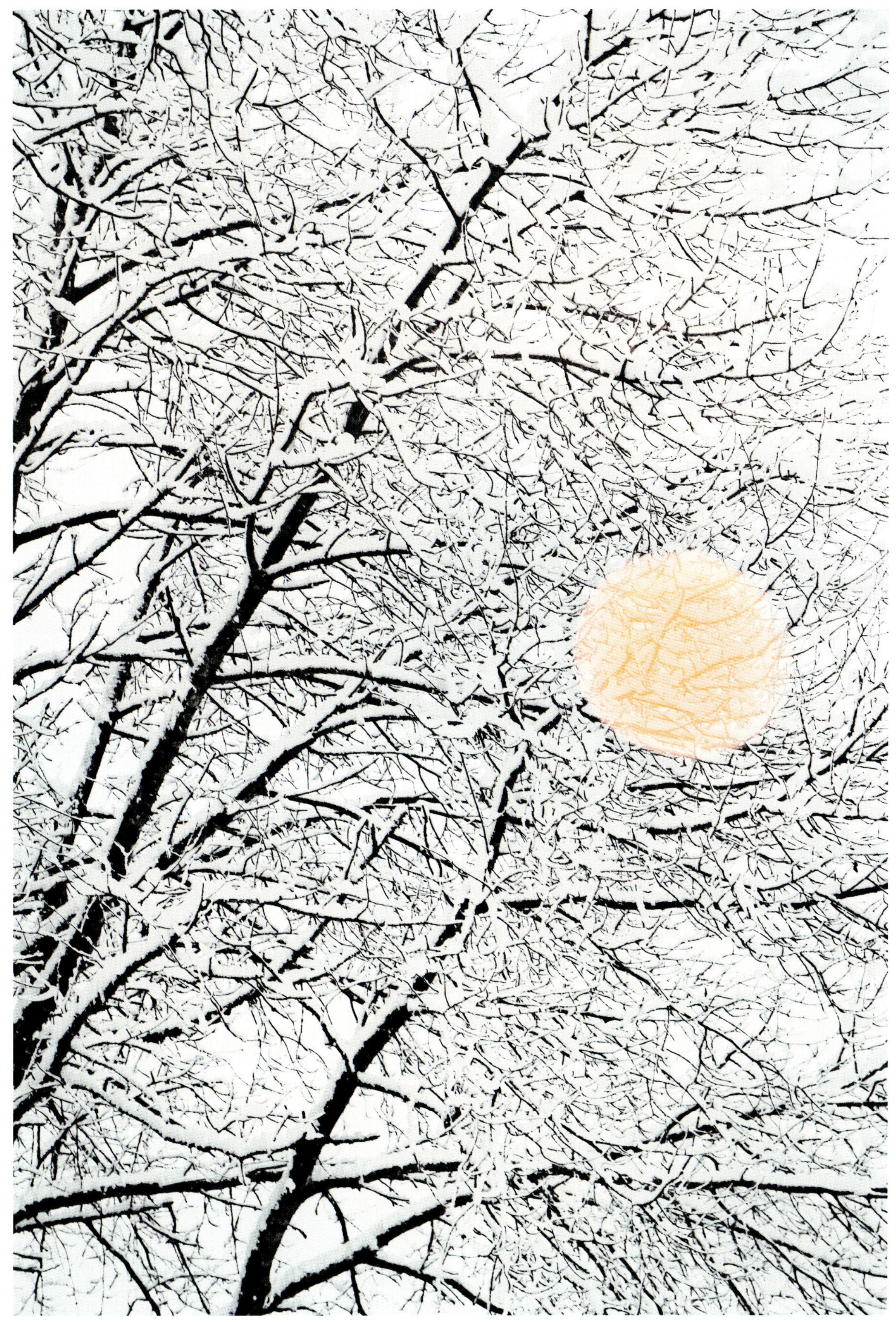

LIST OF WORKS

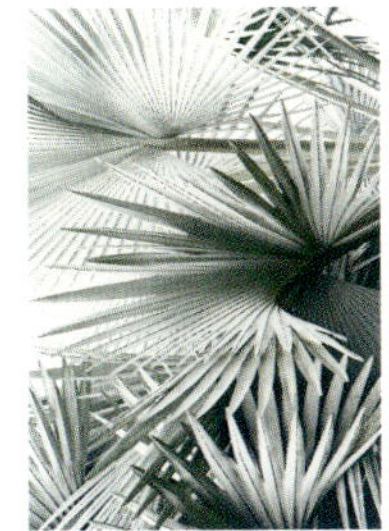

Palm Leaves II, 2019
Imbue Print
Edition of 5 (2 Artist's Proofs)
162.6 × 111.8 cm (64 × 44 in)
Edition of 8 (2 Artist's Proofs)
112 × 78 cm (44.1 × 30.7 in)

Osaka Umbrella, 2017
C-Print
Edition of 8 (2 Artist's Proofs)
50 × 36 cm (19.7 × 14.2 in)

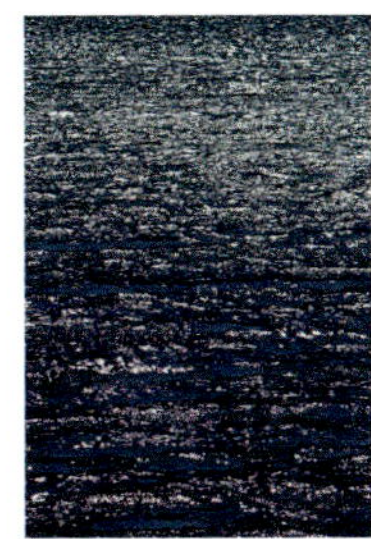

Sea, 2017
Imbue Print on barite paper
Edition of 3 (2 Artist's Proofs)
219.3 × 151 cm (86.3 × 59.5 in)
Edition of 8 (2 Artist's Proofs)
117.3 × 78 cm (46.2 × 30.7 in)

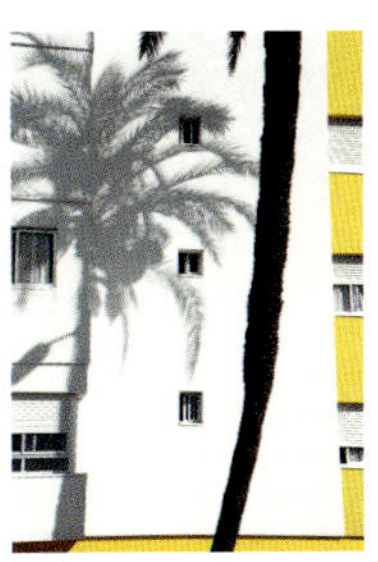

Tarifa, 2018
Imbue Print
Edition of 8 (2 Artist's Proofs)
50 × 36 cm (19.7 × 14.2 in)

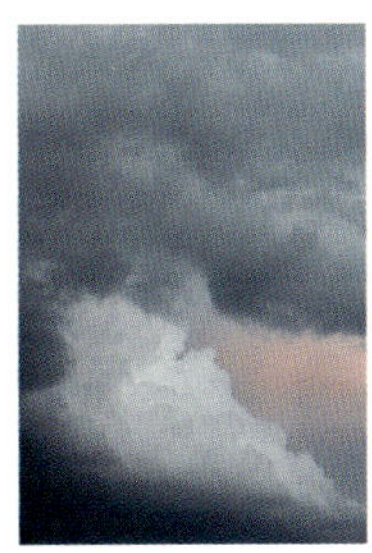

Pink Cloud, 2018
Imbue Print
Edition of 5 (2 Artist's Proofs)
162.6 × 111.8 cm (64 × 44 in)
Edition of 8 (2 Artist's Proofs)
112 × 78 cm (44.1 × 30.7 in)

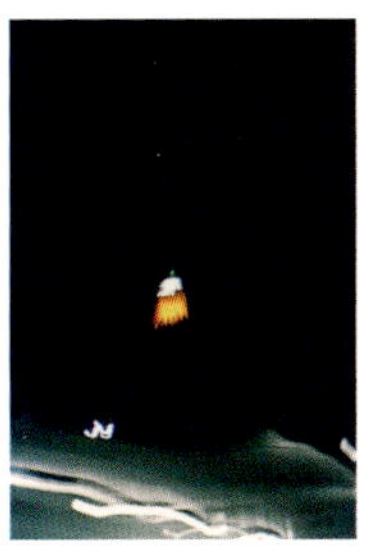

Empire State Building II, 2018
Imbue Print
162.6 × 111.8 cm (64 × 44 in)

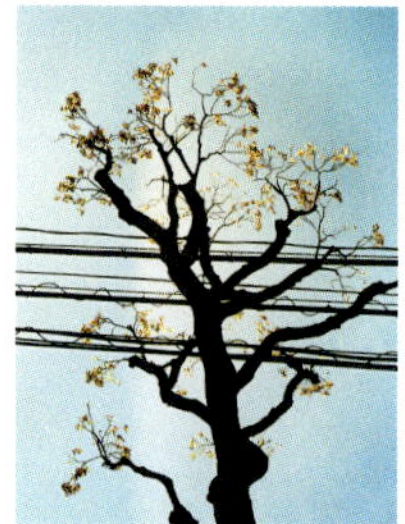

Wire Tree, 2017
C-Print
Edition of 8 (2 Artist's Proofs)
50 × 38 cm (19.7 × 15 in)

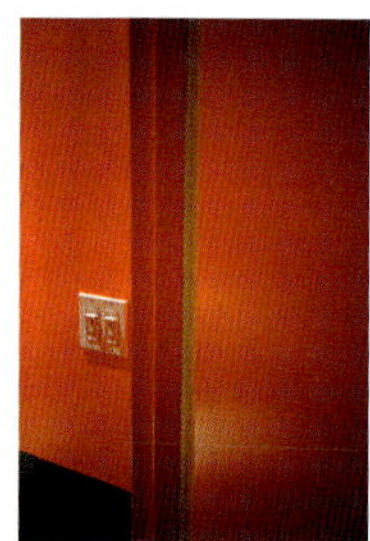

Light Switch, 2018
C-Print
Edition of 8 (2 Artist's Proofs)
71 × 55 cm (22 × 21.7 in)

Palm and a Palm Leaf, 2019
Imbue Print on barite paper
Edition of 8 (2 Artist's Proofs)
71 × 56 cm (27.9 × 22 in)
Edition of 3 (2 Artist's Proofs)
102.4 × 80 cm (40.3 × 31.5 in)

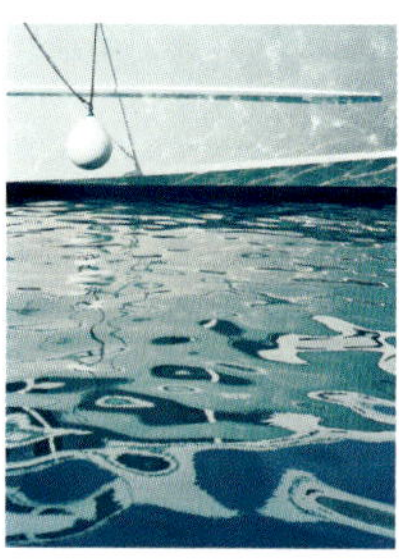

Fender II, 2017
Imbue Print on barite paper
Edition of 5 (2 Artist's Proofs)
164 × 126 cm (64.6 × 49.6 in)

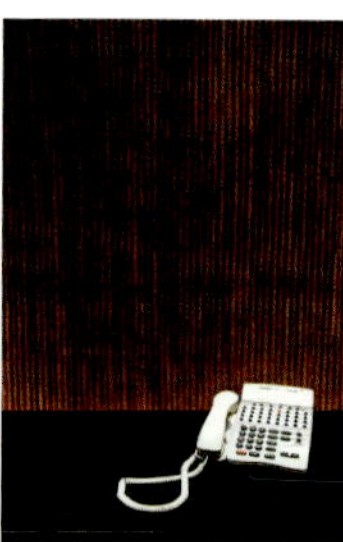

Desk Phone, 2017
C-Print
Edition of 8 (2 Artist's Proofs)
50 × 36 cm (19.7 × 14.2 in)

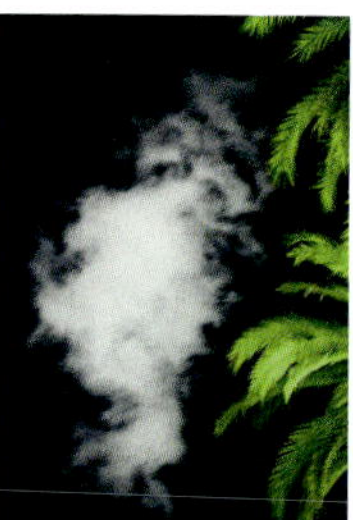

Night Cloud, 2019
Imbue Print
Edition of 5 (2 Artist's Proofs)
162.6 × 111.8 cm (64 × 44 in)
Edition of 8 (2 Artist's Proofs)
112 × 78 cm (44.1 × 30.7 in)

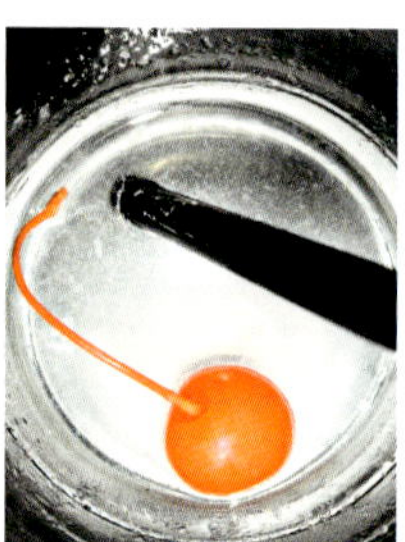

Cherry, 2019
Imbue Print
Edition of 8 (2 Artist's Proofs)
51 × 40.2 cm (20.1 × 15.8 in)

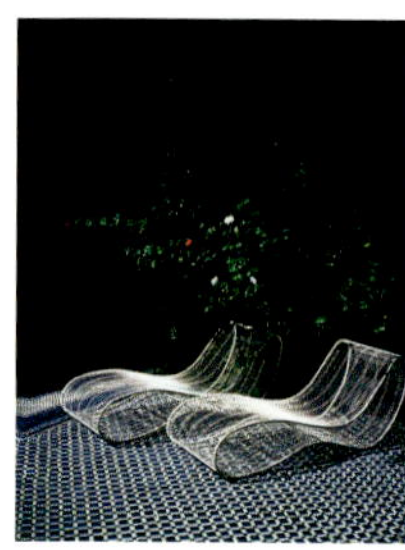

Sunchairs at Night, 2018
C-Print
Edition of 8 (2 Artist's Proofs)
28.6 × 35 cm (11.3 × 13.8 in)

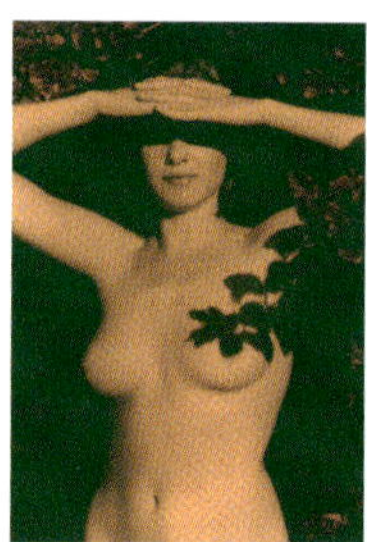

Julie, 2014
Color Print on Arches Vellum
Edition of 5 (2 Artist's Proofs)
153 × 102.8 cm (60.2 × 40.5 in)
Edition of 8 (3 Artist's Proofs)
117.3 × 78 cm (46.2 × 30.7 in)

Wave under a Full Moon, 2015
Imbue Print
Edition of 3 (2 Artist's Proofs)
225 × 150 cm (88.6 × 59.1 in)

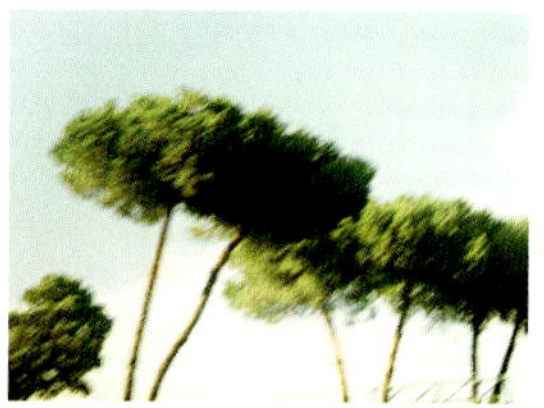

Pine Trees, 2018
Imbue Print on barite paper
Edition of 8 (2 Artist's Proofs)
50 × 63.3 cm (19.7 × 25 in)
Edition of 3 (2 Artist's Proofs)
132.5 × 172 cm (52.2 × 67.7 in)

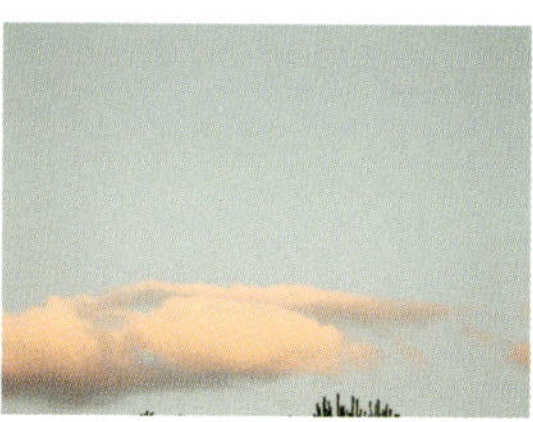

Via Appia, 2018
Imbue Print on barite paper
Edition of 8 (2 Artist's Proofs)
50 × 63.3 cm (19.7 × 25 in)
Edition of 3 (2 Artist's Proofs)
132.5 × 172 cm (52.2 × 67.7 in)

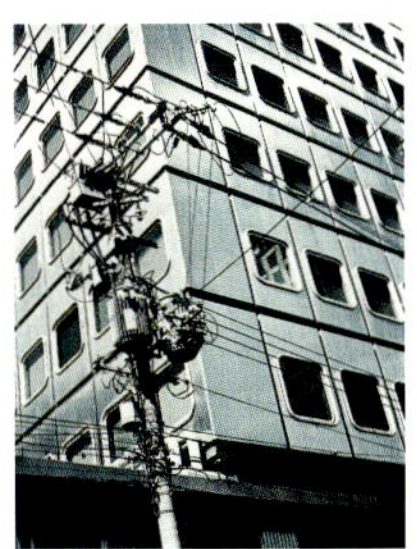

Business Center, 2017
C-Print
Edition of 8 (2 Artist's Proofs)
71 × 55 cm (27.9 × 21.6 in)

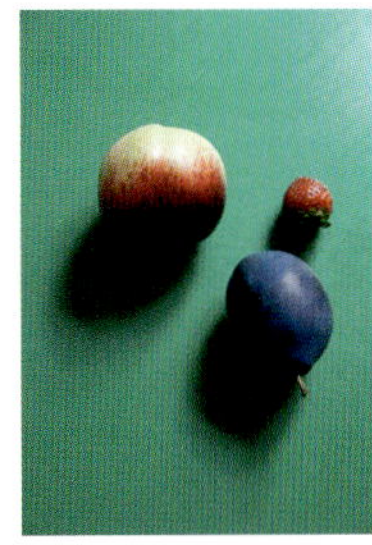

A peach, a plum and a strawberry, 2019
Imbue Print on barite paper
Edition of 8 (2 Artist's Proofs)
35 × 28.6 cm (13.8 × 11.3 in)

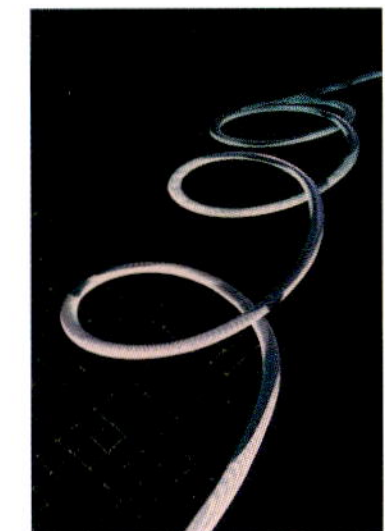

Vacuum Hose, 2019
C-Print
Edition of 5 (2 Artist's Proofs)
162.6 × 111.8 cm (64 × 44 in)

Seville, 2018
Imbue Print on barite paper
Edition of 8 (2 Artist's Proofs)
35 × 25.6 cm (13.8 × 10 in)

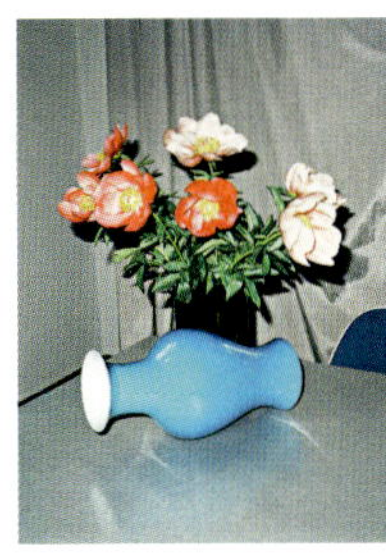

Peonies, a turquoise vase and a blue chair, 2010
Imbue Print
Edition of 5 (2 Artist's Proofs)
71 × 51 cm (28 × 20.1 in)

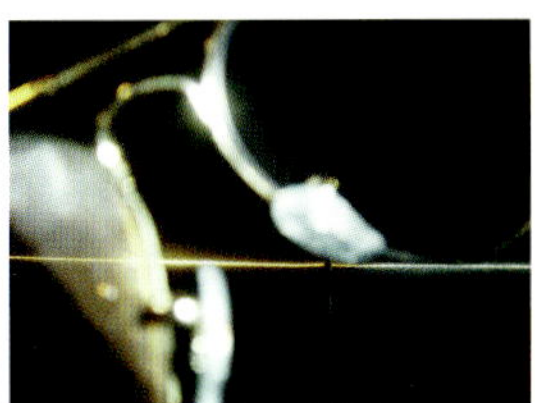

Ray-Ban Series, Four, 2006
Imbue Print on barite paper
Edition of 8 (2 Artist's Proofs)
40.2 × 51 cm (15.8 × 20.1 in)

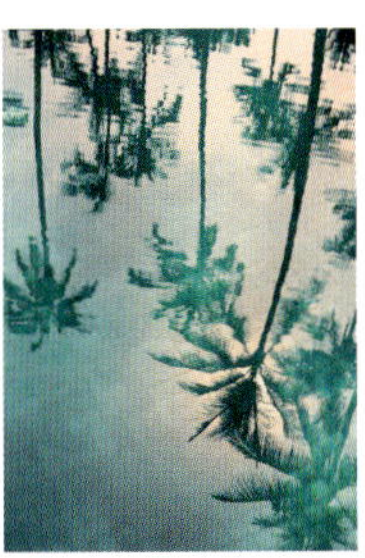

Palms in a Pool, 2017
Imbue Print on barite paper
Edition of 3 (2 Artist's Proofs)
219.3 × 151 cm (86.3 × 59.4 in)
Edition of 8 (2 Artist's Proofs)
117.3 × 82.4 cm (46.2 × 32.4 in)

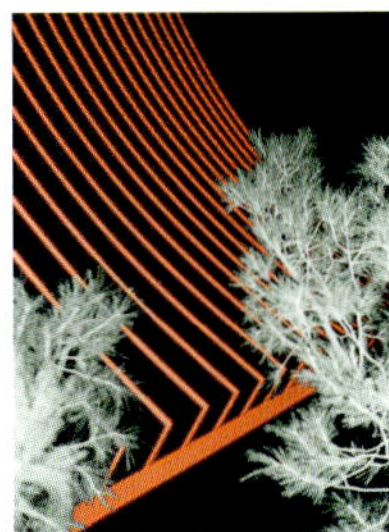

Wynn, 2017
Imbue Print on barite paper
Edition of 8 (2 Artist's Proofs)
35 × 28.6 cm (13.8 × 11.3 in)

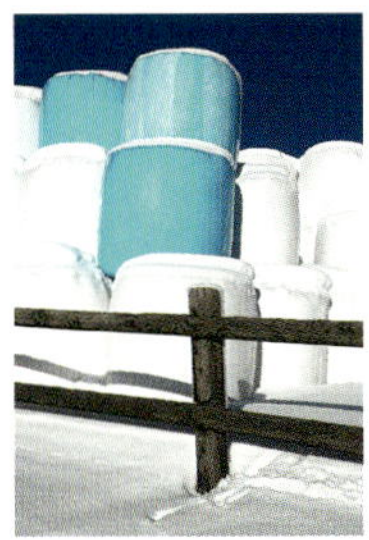

Hay Bales, 2019
Imbue Print
Edition of 8 (2 Artist's Proofs)
50 × 36 cm (19.7 × 14.2 in)

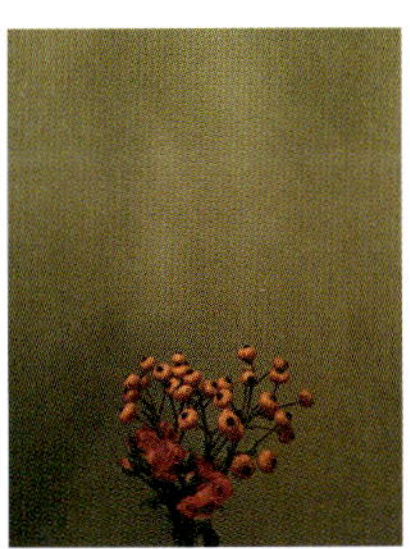

Still Life, 2010
Imbue Print on barite paper
Edition of 8 (2 Artist's Proofs)
35 × 28.6 cm (13.8 × 11.3 in)

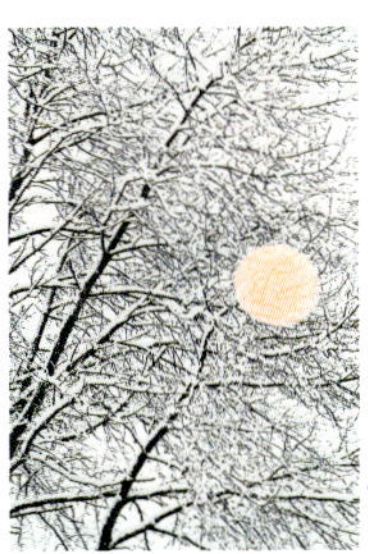

Nippon Tree, 2017
C-Print
Edition of 8 (2 Artist's Proofs)
71 × 55 cm (28 × 21.7 in)

For Lisa, Elliot and Ruben

First edition published in 2021

© 2021 Philipp Keel for the images / All photographs by Philipp Keel
© 2021 Benedict Wells for his text
© 2021 Steidl Publishers for this edition

Editor: Kati Hertzsch
Designer: Kobi Benezri
Translations: Katy Derbyshire
Image Editing: Nora Howald, Oliver Bruns
Color Separations: Steidl image department
Production: Bernard Fischer, Gerhard Steidl
Printing: Steidl, Göttingen

STEIDL
Düstere Str. 4 / 37073 Göttingen, Germany
Phone +49 551 49 60 60
mail@steidl.de
steidl.de

ISBN 978-3-95829-694-7
Printed in Germany by Steidl

www.philippkeel.com